PowerPoint for Lawyers

PAUL J. UNGER

ABA LAW
PRACTICE
DIVISION
The Business of Practicing Law

Cover design by RIPE Creative, Inc.

Figure 1.5(c) TheDoeReport.com

Library of Congress Cataloging-in-Publication Data

Unger, Paul J., author.
   Powerpoint in one hour for lawyers / by Paul J. Unger.
     pages cm
   Includes bibliographical references and index.
   ISBN 978-1-60442-927-5 (alk. paper)
  1. Microsoft PowerPoint (Computer file) 2. Presentation graphics software. 3. Lawyers—United States—Handbooks, manuals, etc. I. American Bar Association. Section of Law Practice Management, sponsoring body. II. Title.
   KF322.5.M53U54   2014
   005.5'8—dc23

2014004177

Contents

About the Author

Paul J. Unger is a national speaker, writer and thought-leader in the legal technology industry. He is an attorney and founding principal of Affinity Consulting Group, a nationwide consulting company providing legal technology consulting, continuing legal education, and training.

He is the Chair of the ABA Legal Technology Resource Center Board (www.lawtechnology.org/), former Chair of ABA TECHSHOW (2011) (www.techshow.com), member of the American Bar Association, Columbus Bar Association, Ohio State Bar Association, Ohio Association for Justice, and Central Ohio Association for Justice. He specializes in trial presentation and litigation technology, document and case management, paperless office strategies, and legal-specific software training for law firms and legal departments throughout the Midwest. Mr. Unger has provided trial presentation consultation for over 400 cases and is an Adjunct Professor for Capital University Law School's Paralegal Program. In his spare time, he likes to run and restore historic homes.

PowerPoint in One Hour

PowerPoint is a full-featured slide-show presentation tool that helps lawyers efficiently create professional-looking slide shows and then deliver them to clients, participants in continuing legal education seminars, or a trier of fact or law in a hearing, mediation, or trial. Lawyers can use PowerPoint to do the following:

- explain a complex legal concept
- introduce a medical term or procedure
- bolster arguments by adding images, graphics, or text
- build quasi animations to explain a process or re-create an event
- convey numeric data in visually compelling graphics
- present an opening statement or a closing argument
- supplement expert witness testimony
- play back video and/or video-recorded depositions

While PowerPoint has been around for a long time, its use and misuse have evolved. In the 1990s, lawyers often had slides and bullet points for every thought or idea, resulting in bloated presentations full of text and too many details. We cited research indicating that people are much more likely to remember information that they see as well as hear. While theoretically true, it also created information overload.

What follows is a discussion on the proper and improper use of PowerPoint and the concept of storyboarding. You see, as useful as PowerPoint can be, it can also easily be misused or abused and result in some pretty terrible presentations. These principles will guide you down the right path of creating and delivering dynamic and professional presentations to your audience.

The Slide Story— Storyboarding Made Easy

Images and headlines are glued together by your story.

—Paul J. Unger, Esq.

Hans Hofmann, the late renowned German-born American artist and teacher of art, once said, "The ability to simplify means to eliminate the unnecessary so that the necessary may speak." I believe it is vital that we live by this principle when we create PowerPoint presentations.

Storyboarding is a process whereby illustrations or images are displayed in sequence for the purpose of visualizing animation or the motion of a picture or graphic. It allows the storytellers to discuss and develop ways of presenting a narrative. Historically, storyboards have been used to develop screenplays, movies, television programs, comic strips, and other similar forms of media.

Presenters and lawyers in the courtroom have borrowed from this traditional concept and, with the use of PowerPoint, put their own twist on storyboarding. When we talk about storyboarding in the context of PowerPoint, I generally think of two terms: *storyboarding,* the process, and a *storyboard,* the graphic.

The storyboarding process helps us develop the narrative visually and creatively. The actual storyboards are used in the process. However, in the courtroom with PowerPoint, the storyboards are carefully selected graphics, images, or headlines that are used during the presentation to enhance or supplement the story. Stated another way, the storyboards are a series of visual frames, which, when put together in a particular order, convey a visual story. They often show the "big picture."

In the context of PowerPoint presentations, I use the two terms (*storyboarding* and *storyboard*) loosely to mean carefully selected graphics used to develop a narrative into something visual that others can more easily understand. In the courtroom or in a client presentation, however, storyboarding requires more than just a series of graphics or slides. Without a good story and the skill/art to actually tell it, the storyboards by themselves are meaningless.

The technique of storyboarding is incredibly compatible with the development of PowerPoint presentations by legal professionals. By now, you have probably seen hundreds of bad PowerPoint presentations riddled with boring slides filled with bullet points and text in "outline" formats. PowerPoint storyboarding cures this ailment and allows a presenter to use PowerPoint frames to display graphics that actually help complement a story without distracting the audience by making them read text. Leave the text or outlines in your notes or memorize them. Don't put them in the slides! Using Presenter view in PowerPoint is one way to help achieve this goal (see the later lesson on Dual Monitor and Presenter View).

Cliff Atkinson, in his book *Beyond Bullet Points: Using Microsoft® PowerPoint® to Create Presentations that Inform, Motivate, and Inspire,* discusses in good detail the concepts of sensory memory, working memory, and long-term memory. In a nutshell, Atkinson explains that many presentations overload the working memory. This overload has damaging consequences on listeners' retention and on their ability to solve problems. When presented with too much information in a slide, often in the form of text, their minds go into overdrive while trying to reconcile the spoken word with the information on the slide. When this happens, Atkinson explains, information is lost. His and others' research helps guide presenters in understanding how to use multimedia in a way that best promotes effective learning.

Some of this research, including my own informal research, is discussed in this book. However, for a more in-depth look at this information and those who have inspired my theories and practice, see the following resources:

- Cliff Atkinson, *Beyond Bullet Points: Using Microsoft® PowerPoint® to Create Presentations that Inform, Motivate, and Inspire* (Redmond, WA: Microsoft Press, 2011).
- Cliff Atkinson, "The Cognitive Load of PowerPoint: Q&A with Richard E. Mayer," MarketingProfs, March 16, 2004, http://www.marketingprofs.com/4/atkinson10.asp.
- Richard E. Mayer, ed. *The Cambridge Handbook of Multimedia Learning* (New York: Cambridge University Press, 2005).
- Garr Reynolds, *Presentation Zen: Simple Ideas on Presentation Design and Delivery* Second Edition (Berkeley: New Riders, 2012).

Sample Storyboard

Figure 1.1 shows an example of PowerPoint storyboarding in a case involving a slip and fall on an unnatural accumulation of ice and snow. This follows precisely the definition above: images and headlines glued together by a narrative. Not a single bullet point exists in this opening statement. There absolutely could have been a few bullet points scattered throughout, but it just wasn't necessary in this particular presentation.

Figure 1.1 PowerPoint Storyboarding

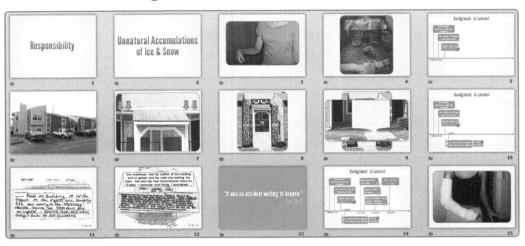

James Arnold, the lawyer arguing this case, wanted to tell a story in plain English, using concise slides and graphics. Arnold began with a neutral statement about one of the themes in the case: responsibility. He then transitioned into a neutral statement about the law in Ohio regarding the duty to remove man-made or unnatural accumulations of ice and snow. Simple headlines were used for these (see Figure 1.2) as a more detailed explanation was provided verbally.

Figure 1.2 Headline Slides

Next, Arnold started telling the story about the injured plaintiff. Within two to three minutes of the opening slide, keeping the jury engaged with good storytelling techniques reinforced by the storyboards, Arnold moved into exactly how and why the plaintiff was injured. This occurred within the first four slides.

In this case, it was important to demonstrate that the apartment complex removed the gutters from the apartment building but left the diverter on the roof and then failed to replace the gutters before the winter months arrived. Consequently, as ice and snow on the roof melted during the day when the sun was out, water would hit the diverter, run directly over the edge of the roof, and then freeze on the sidewalk in the only areas where one could enter and exit the building (see the two slides in Figure 1.3 below).

Figure 1.3 Slides Demonstrating Events

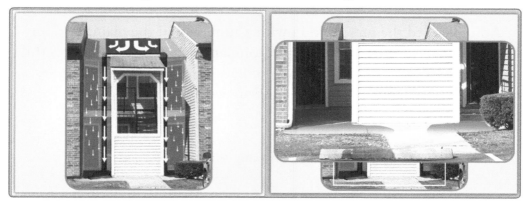

Arnold and his team next needed to establish that the landlord had notice of the situation. In slides, they displayed a series of work orders showing complaints about the dangerous man-made icy condition. On each slide where they showed a document, they used a callout to blow up and highlight the important part of the document. An example is shown in Figure 1.4 below. (This is critical because the text on any document is almost always too small to read if one sizes the document to fit on the slide. Document callouts and highlighting are covered in Lesson 14.)

Figure 1.4 Document Slide with Callout and Highlight

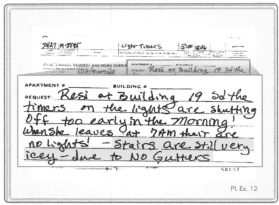

Arnold ended the presentation with a summary of the plaintiff's injuries (see slide in Figure 1.5 below), accompanied by a brief but impactful introduction of the catastrophic economic and non-economic damages in this case. Arguably, the trial was already won by the end of this opening statement.

Figure 1.5 Slide Showing Plaintiff Injuries

In PowerPoint's Normal view, shown in Figure 1.6 below, along the left you see the storyboards, and below the larger image you see the narrative that accompanies that particular storyboard. The narrative (or notes) is visible in PowerPoint's Presenter view and allows the presenter to keep unnecessary text out of the slides. In many cases, especially this one, the words needed to be spoken, and *not* lengthy sentences or bullet points on the slide itself. Remember our definition of a storyboard: *images or head-lines glued together by your story.*

Figure 1.6 PowerPoint Normal View

Effects of PowerPoint Storyboarding on Memory

This summary describes an informal study that examines the effect that PowerPoint has on memory. I found that when one focus group had the benefit of viewing PowerPoint slides in the form of storyboards (images or headlines glued together by a story, or a short list of bullet points in the form of headlines) while hearing an oral presentation, participants remembered significantly more information than those in a focus group that did not have the benefit of viewing the PowerPoint. These initial results have implications for not only the use of PowerPoint but also its effectiveness.

Many lawyers tend to use PowerPoint as an outline or a teleprompter. The end result for the speaker may be a smoother presentation, but the end result for the listeners may be quite the opposite. This typically leads to presenters misusing PowerPoint or not using it at all because of its perceived ineffectiveness.

I believe there is a middle ground, so I tested the impact of PowerPoint storyboarding on memory. If listeners could remember more information with storyboards, lawyers could use storyboarding to benefit their audience, not just themselves. Moreover, more lawyers would be willing to use PowerPoint instead of shying away from it because of its rumored lack of usefulness.

Method

Participants: Ninety-six lawyers attending a CLE presentation on courtroom technology at the Ohio State Bar Association participated in this informal study.

Procedure: Participants were not aware that they were going to take part in the study. In the beginning of the session, they were informed that they would be listening to a ten-minute "opening statement" and then given a quiz. One-half of the participants exited the conference hall, and the other half remained. I read the first group (Group A) a prepared opening statement verbatim, accompanied by a PowerPoint presentation consisting of slides in the form of headlines and images—storyboards. It is important to note that no additional information was presented in the slides. There were pictures, documents, and a few bullet points, but only information contained in the oral presentation. No additional data or words were displayed on the slides.

After presenting to Group A, I thanked and dismissed them. I then brought Group B into the conference hall and read the same opening statement verbatim; however, this time I read it *without* the accompanying PowerPoint storyboard slides. In other words, Group B received a pure oral presentation.

Finally I invited Group A back into the conference hall and administered a ten-question quiz to both groups about the information conveyed during the presentation. Only three or four minutes had passed since Group B (oral only) had heard the opening statement. Nearly fifteen minutes had passed since Group A (oral and PowerPoint) had heard the opening statement.

Results

Group A's average score was 7.75 out of 10. Group B's average score was 4.25 out of 10.

One question had four parts, giving 25 percent of a single point to each correct answer. The question asked participants to list as many of the four facts as they could remember about what Dr. Jones was going to testify about to the jury. Group A, who had the benefit of the PowerPoint storyboards, recalled three out of four. Group B, who didn't have the benefit of the storyboards, recalled one out of four.

Discussion and Lessons Learned

Listeners remember more information when an oral presentation is accompanied by PowerPoint storyboards. We know from this informal study that listeners clearly recalled more information about a presentation when it was delivered with PowerPoint slides. The difference was significant. The group who had the benefit of PowerPoint scored 75 percent; those who didn't have the benefit of PowerPoint scored 42.5 percent.

Using PowerPoint storyboards is an effective way to deliver information. PowerPoint storyboarding, which is the use of images or headlines glued together by a speaker's narrative, proved in this study to be an effective method of presenting information. While we don't have data to compare this method with a so-called bad PowerPoint presentation—full of text and outlining—at a very minimum, we know it is better than using nothing at all.

Tips for Effective Use of PowerPoint

Don't Overuse PowerPoint

No technology replaces the vividness of one's own imagination! You do not need a graphic or slide for every single thought or idea. This can water down your message and overload the jury with verbal and visual information. Always ask yourself, "Does this slide advance the ball, or is it better to state the information?"

Don't Misuse PowerPoint

PowerPoint's misuse is a nationwide epidemic. Critics of PowerPoint, like Edward R. Tufte, say that the program itself facilitates the making of bad presentations. Moreover, Tufte claims that PowerPoint "stupefies" our culture by encouraging fragmented thinking through bullet points and linear slides, further diminishing our attention span, and feeding us heaping spoonfuls of graphic sugar.[1] While I see Tufte's point, I think PowerPoint is just a tool that humans use or misuse. When a tailor sews a crooked seam, should we blame the sewing machine? If a presenter has poor content and bad graphics or does not communicate clearly,

---

1. Edward R. Tufte, *The Cognitive Style of PowerPoint* (Cheshire, CT: Graphics Press, 2003).

should we blame PowerPoint? The bottom line is that if used properly, PowerPoint is an extremely effective tool to deliver information to our fast-paced world.

Speak with Passion, Not PowerPoint

One critic recently asked, "Could you imagine if Martin Luther King Jr. gave his famous 'I Have a Dream' speech using PowerPoint?" If your goal is to persuade and motivate, then give a speech and scale back on the use of PowerPoint or other computer graphics. If your goal is to persuade and *educate*, then it is OK to use PowerPoint if you use it correctly.

Use Plain English in Your Speech and Graphics

Use plain English that everyone understands. This is still one of the biggest mistakes that lawyers make. Instead of saying, "This litigation is before us today because the defendant failed to exercise ordinary care in his relationship as a physician with the plaintiff, and such failure was the proximate cause of the plaintiff's damages," simply say, "A doctor must do what other doctors would do in a similar situation." Cut the jargon out of your presentations and say things an average person would understand.

Use PowerPoint to Educate the Jury in Voir Dire and Opening Statement

Jurors are pretty street-smart, but when it comes to science and numbers, you may want to provide some tutoring up front! It is estimated that, sadly, less than half of the jury will have math skills better than performing basic one-step calculations. Create a visual glossary to explain terms that will be used in the trial.

Don't make the mistake of assuming that your expert will educate the jury for you. Make a road map for the jury so they can spend more time on understanding and analyzing your expert's position than on learning a new complex vocabulary.

Figure 2.1 is a very simple example of just one slide used to explain a TIA (transient ischemic attack), or ministroke. Avoid the bullet point definitions or a full paragraph of text, and use headlines and graphics, glued together by your narrative.

Figure 2.1 Slide Used to Explain TIA

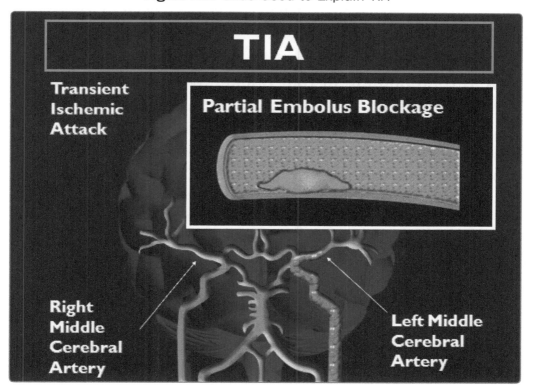

We did not create a text-based slide to define TIA or its symptoms. We could have, but felt that the visual, accompanied by good storytelling, was much more effective. We showed the slide and then *verbally* informed the jury that a transient ischemic attack is a stroke that lasts only a few minutes—that is what *transient* means. It occurs when the blood supply to part of the brain is briefly interrupted—that is what *ischemic* means ("decrease or interruption in blood flow"). Further, we explained that TIA symptoms, which usually occur suddenly, are similar to those of stroke but do not last as long and can include numbness or weakness in the face, arm, or leg, especially on one side of the body; confusion or difficulty in talking or understanding speech; trouble with vision in one or both eyes; difficulty with walking or dizziness; and loss of balance and coordination.

Have Strong Content in Your Spoken Words, Slides, and Written Materials

PowerPoint cannot mask the fact that a case or a presentation stinks. Edward Tufte argues in his essay *The Cognitive Style of PowerPoint*[2] that it is easy to let PowerPoint shorten evidence and thought; organize complex information in a single-path model template; break up narrative and data into minimal fragments; decorate and fluff a slide show with format, not content; and promote an attitude of commercialism that turns everything into a sales pitch. All of these "evils" diminish content. I have personally witnessed thousands of good *and* bad presentations, and content and clear delivery dictated their success . . . *not* PowerPoint.

Don't Dilute Your Message with Too Many Bullet Point Lists

Bullet point lists are overused and are too verbose, but that doesn't mean they should never be included. If done properly, they can be a helpful

---

2. Ibid., 4.

tool. I recommend a minimal number of bullet point slides; when creating them, think of the bullet points as headlines or titles about a main thought or idea (see Figure 2.2). The substance *behind* the bullet point is delivered orally and/or in written materials (or trial exhibits). The key to making bullet points effective is to use them sparingly.

An example of using bullet points effectively would be to have a slide that summarizes a witness's key testimony in the form of headline bullet points animated to appear one point at a time. This is a good format if used occasionally. Furthermore, a juror would be able to listen to the presenter and also comprehend the bullet points because the slide isn't too much to reconcile with the spoken word.

Figure 2.2 Slide with Bullet Points

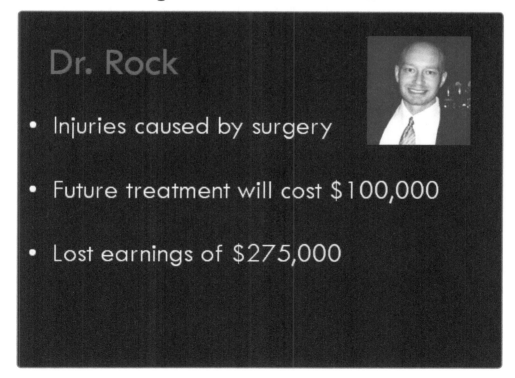

Focus on Clear Delivery

Steps to Creating a Successful Presentation Supplemented by PowerPoint

1. Develop excellent content and handout materials.
2. Practice the clear delivery of that content.
3. Prepare your PowerPoint storyboard slides based on what you need in steps 1 and 2.
4. Practice, revise, practice, revise, and practice *with* the technology!

Steps to Creating a Bad Presentation Supplemented by PowerPoint

1. Prepare your PowerPoint slides.
2. Speak from your PowerPoint slides.

PowerPoint can fragment the presentation of thoughts and data *if you let it*. Any visual aids can fragment a presentation if you don't "own it psychologically" and know how to transition smoothly through your visuals. This is why you should first write or outline the content of your speech. The second step is to focus on practicing its clear delivery. The last step should be to create your PowerPoint slides *based on what you need for the content and delivery*. In other words, think about what visuals can best help you clearly tell your story, and then use PowerPoint or other tools to build and present those visuals. The story comes before the storyboards. The storyboards then build your PowerPoint.

If the Slide Is a Distraction, You Are Missing the "Point"!

The whole purpose of PowerPoint is to make a point—not a distraction. Avoid the overuse of animation, sound effects, and cheesy backgrounds. This is what gives PowerPoint a bad name! Animations and bad flashy backdrops can be very distracting, which obviously diminishes your presentation and your credibility. This doesn't mean that your presentation shouldn't look like a million bucks. Hire an artist to create an *original* background that is professional looking and that no one else has seen. Pick one or two effects to bring in text and graphics, and stick with just those effects. I recommend the "fade" effect. It is very professional, tasteful, and not at all distracting.

Unless you are just starting to use PowerPoint, try to avoid the standard design templates. Most people have seen these templates and graphics dozens of times, if not more. Try to create graphics that give you a unique and professional brand. A great way to do this is to contact a local art school and hire a student. Tell the school that you are looking to create a PowerPoint backdrop for your company's presentations. Ask the student to create a JPG and then to produce a theme or POTX template that you can load into your PowerPoint templates folder.

Here are some other excellent sources for PowerPoint design templates:

1. **Digital Juice** (www.digitaljuice.com) is a suite of thousands of PowerPoint backdrops and royalty-free graphics, clip art, sounds, and animation.
2. **Microsoft Office** (http://office.microsoft.com/en-us/templates) publishes free templates that you can download.
3. **Sonia Coleman's Digital Studio** (http://www.soniacoleman.com) has a nice library of free templates and tutorials.

Design, Color, and Layout Are Important

Design conservatively and with professionalism. Most of the time you should use darker backgrounds (such as dark blue, green, etc.) and high-contrasting color text (such as white, yellow, etc.). A white background is OK, but if you don't know what you are doing, it can be too bright. Also remember to be color-blind friendly. One in ten people have problems interpreting color. Avoid the combined use of red and green, green and yellow, and blue and yellow.

Does Color Matter?

Yes, color does matter, but only in the sense that the presentation must appear professional. My real-life experience, backed by focus group research, indicates that as long as the slide is professional in appearance and easy to read/see (admittedly, a subjective standard), jurors don't care if it has a green, blue, or black background. Furthermore, my research has shown that color used in a PowerPoint slide show in the context of a trial does not affect memory retention. Jurors pay more attention to the merits of the case and delivery than to the aesthetics of a slide presentation. Although the failure to use PowerPoint or some other visual memory-reinforcing aid may affect memory retention, color generally doesn't make a significant impact.

The exception to this is when you deviate from a color scheme. Say you use white text on a blue background in a twenty-slide presentation, but you decide to use yellow text on a blue background on the tenth slide. That will indeed have a positive impact on memory retention. However, it could easily be argued that the same effect could be accomplished by changing the font or underlining.

Does Size Matter? Remember 8H!

Text not clearly readable by everyone adds frustration and creates a distraction. I've seen too many presenters say, "You may not be able to read this, but . . ." If that is the case, then why even show the slide?

One old rule of thumb in the presentation industry is called the 8H rule of legibility. The rule was developed as a guideline when 35 mm slides were in use, and it goes like this: if you can read an image from eight times its height, odds are that everyone will be able to read it when projected.

In those days, if you could read a 35 mm slide, which was 1 inch in height, from 8 inches away, that slide would be legible under most presentation conditions.

Figure 2.3 8H Rule Illustrated

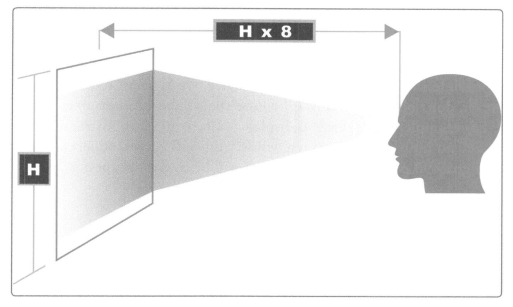

Translated to today's world, if your computer screen is 10 inches in height, scoot away from your screen 80 inches. If you can read the image on the screen, then everyone in an audience should probably be able to see it when it's projected.

In practical terms, that means you should never go below 11-point type. I think 18 is a safer number, but obviously 22 or 24 gives you extra wiggle room in case the presentation screen is a little smaller and farther away than you expected.

Use Fonts That Are Easy to Read

Avoid Courier and Times New Roman fonts. Instead use fonts like Calibri, Twentieth Century Monotype, Tahoma, Arial, and Helvetica. They are easier to read from longer distances.

Give the Audience Extra Space on Your Slides— Cut the Clutter!

Avoid information overload. Your slides and graphics should not be too cluttered. If you must use bullet points, try to limit bullets to three or four per slide with no more than ten to twelve words on a single slide. However, don't obsess over this. Of course there are exceptions to every rule. For example, if you want to display a statute or a jury instruction, how can you limit that slide to ten words? You can't. If you adhere to these general goals 90 percent of the time, you will be in great shape.

Mix Up the Media

Remember to use whiteboards, chalkboards, easels, and enlarged pictures from time to time. There are two main reasons for this. First, jurors can become bored with PowerPoint and a screen just as easily as they can with a chalkboard. We know from the television industry that changing the frequency of angle shots within the same visual scene improves memory recognition. Count the number of angle changes within a visual scene in a sitcom from the 1960s versus a sitcom (or reality show) created today. This teaches us that people quickly become bored. So mix up the media.

The second major reason for not relying 100 percent on PowerPoint is that occasionally you want an illustration, a time line, or a photograph sitting on an easel for a long period of time so the jury can look at it for clarification or other reasons. If you have a blowup, you can set it out and also show PowerPoint slides.

Don't Read Slides or Use PowerPoint as an Outline

Many people believe that it is appropriate to read PowerPoint slides or use them as an outline. I respectfully submit to these people that they have been led down the wrong road. It is OK to use a slide here and there to remind you of an important topic. However, there is a big difference between that and creating slides with outline numbering and long lists. Don't do it. It is lazy, grossly ineffective, and painful to watch as an observer. Your message gets lost in all the needless slides and text.

Backup, Backup, Backup!

In smaller dollar cases that cannot justify the expense of a trial presentation consultant, the biggest mistake I see is failing to bring a backup computer, external USB hard drive, or projector. When things go wrong, as they sometimes do, you *must* have backup equipment. Good rule of thumb: bring two of everything.

Someone Else Should Run the Presentation

For a CLE program, if you are just using PowerPoint, it is fairly easy to run the presentation yourself if you are familiar with the software. You may want to bring an IT person or assistant with you a time or two until you become comfortable enough to do it on your own. Nowadays, so many people know PowerPoint that you can probably find a volunteer or an audiovisual coordinator to help you. Don't bank on it though. You should learn enough to at least be able add or remove slides, make textual changes, and connect the laptop to the projector before you fly solo.

For a courtroom presentation, it is a mistake to operate the PowerPoint yourself. Running the technology while acting as a trial lawyer is asking for trouble. Whether it be a paralegal or a consultant that you hire, whatever you do, don't run the presentation on your own. Being in the trenches of high-tech trials on a weekly basis for over fifteen years, I can honestly say that at least one potential disaster occurs each month. These issues should be invisible to the lawyers, jurors, and judge! You have enough to deal with trying to hit 90 to 100 percent of the important issues in the case. The last thing you need to worry about is a failing hard drive or a bad bulb in your LCD projector. Delegate these worries to someone else!

It's Never Too Early to Get Training

Lawyers are textbook procrastinators. You cannot wait until one month before trial to become proficient with software that is going to either make or break you. There are fantastic training programs available in every major city. Get your training out of the way four to six months before you need to use PowerPoint, and think about using a professional to hold your hand through your first presentation.

Get Approval from the Court in Advance

If your presentation is in the courtroom, exercise professionalism and get permission from the court in advance. You clearly do not have to expose your entire game plan. Simply tell the court at the appropriate time that you may want to display some evidence through PowerPoint. Ask if this will be OK.

Treat the Court Staff and Courtroom with Respect

Would you walk into the judge's private office and start rearranging the furniture? Would you set up a 10-foot movie screen? Definitely not, unless you had a death wish. So don't do it in the courtroom without first making friends and consulting with the judge, bailiff, court reporter, court clerk, or others who use that room as an office on a daily basis. Think about how you would feel if someone just walked in your office and started rearranging things.

Three Final Rules for Using Technology in the Courtroom

1. Have something meaningful to present.
2. Forget what you learned in law school and say things the average person would understand.
3. No technology in the world is going to help you with Rules 1 and 2!

Now let's get to work!

PowerPoint 101

Working with the User Interface

As an expert PowerPoint 2003 (and earlier) user moving to PowerPoint 2007 and 2010, I found it challenging at first to figure out where everything was in the new versions. I felt like I showed up at the grocery store and the aisles had been moved. All the food was there, but in completely new places.

Once I became acclimated, I actually liked the new interface a lot better than the old one. A sample of the basic interface for PowerPoint 2010 is shown in Figure 3.1. The general consensus is clearly that the new interface is better and users really like it, especially those who are brand-new to the program. Users who knew the older interface will simply have to invest more time deprogramming themselves from the old way of doing things.

PowerPoint 2010 Basic Interface Terminology

Figure 3.1 PowerPoint 2010 Basic Interface

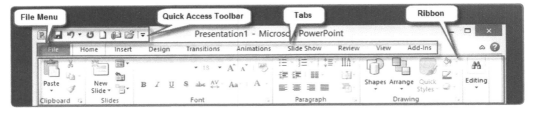

File Menu

The **File** menu (see Figure 3.2) is used to **Save**, **Save As**, **Open**, **Close**, **Print**, **Exit**, and change Options and Add-Ins. It replaced the dreaded and failed **Office** button in PowerPoint 2007.

Figure 3.2 File Menu

Quick Access Toolbar

Use and modify the Quick Access Toolbar (QAT) to store your most frequently used commands. By default, the Quick Access Toolbar is configured with three options: save, undo, and redo/repeat typing. To modify and customize the QAT, click on the drop-down arrow located on the far right side of the QAT, as shown in Figure 3.3, and select the available commands or *More Commands*, which will display hundreds of other choices. By adding functions to the QAT, you can perform them with one mouse click.

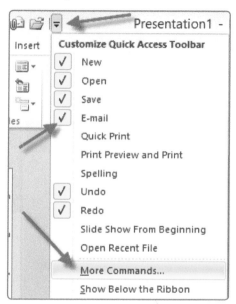

Figure 3.3 Customization Menu for Quick Access Toolbar

Tabs

The tabs are located at the top of the screen, immediately below the title bar, and they replace the old menu bar. (The tabs section is labeled on Figure 3.1.) Tabs work similarly to the menu bars in Office 2003 and earlier, except instead of listing different menus that are text based and nested (sometimes hard to find), the ribbons have larger buttons with icons and labels so finding commands should be much easier (see the **Paste** button in Figure 3.4).

Ribbon

Ribbons have replaced most menus and toolbars and contain (almost) all of the commands that are used to format a slide. Each ribbon contains a group of related commands and functions. There are nine main ribbons that are always present (see the tabs shown in Figure 3.1) and multiple ribbons that only appear with a contextual tab.

Commands on ribbons are arranged into groups. Groups contain a variety of buttons, launchers, and galleries. The Paragraph group on the **Home** ribbon is shown in Figure 3.4.

Not every command is displayed in the ribbon. Extra options for a group can be accessed by clicking a launcher (labeled in Figure 3.4). The launcher will "launch" a dialog with additional options and controls. In addition, a button may have a downward-pointing arrow (triangle) that provides more choices. I often refer to these as drop-down menus (see the example on the **Paste** button in Figure 3.4). Finally, extra options can be accessed by right-clicking on any button on a ribbon.

Figure 3.4 Elements of PowerPoint Home Ribbon

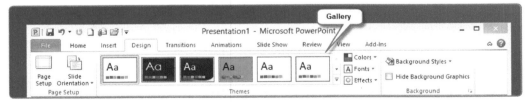

Galleries are groups of samples showing a preview of the formatting that will be applied by clicking a sample. (A gallery for the **Design** ribbon is shown in Figure 3.5) Hovering over a gallery sample will cause PowerPoint to display a "live preview" of the formatting in the document without actually applying the change.

Figure 3.5 Formatting Gallery

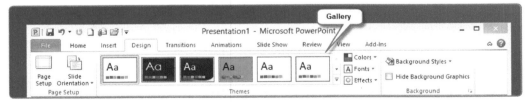

Contextual Tabs and Ribbon

Contextual tabs are tabs that appear based on what you have selected in the main PowerPoint slide. For example, there is a **Picture Tools** contextual tab that appears only if you have a picture selected (see Figure 3.6). The beauty of contextual tabs is that they appear automatically and provide you with every imaginable tool to edit the object you're working on (table, graphic, etc.). The aggravating part of contextual tabs is that if you don't have an object selected, you may never find the function you are trying to perform.

Figure 3.6 Picture Tools Tab on Ribbon

Inserting a New Blank Slide

From the **Home** ribbon, select the drop-down menu from the **New Slide** button. A series of layouts will appear (see Figure 3.7). Select the desired layout.

Figure 3.7 New Slide Layout Options

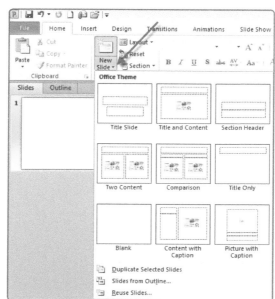

Duplicating an Existing Slide

Often when creating a PowerPoint slide, you have already assembled similar slides in the presentation. Tap into those slides to save time. This is especially true if creating a series of complex slides to build a time line or describe a process. You can make a new slide based on an existing slide in your presentation. Don't reinvent the wheel! If you need to create a new slide similar to one you already have, use the Duplicate Selected Slides feature.

Select the slide that you want to duplicate. From the **Home** ribbon, select the drop-down menu from the **New Slide** button.

Figure 3.8 Duplicating Slides

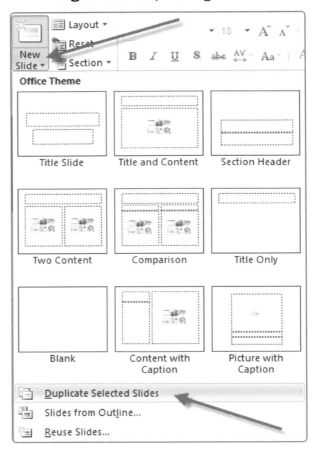

Select ***Duplicate Selected Slides*** as shown in Figure 3.8.

Once inserted, you can move the slide to a different position by dragging and dropping the thumbnail located in the Normal or Slide Sorter view (see Figure 3.9), and edit the slide as needed.

Inserting a Slide from Another Presentation

When creating a PowerPoint presentation, you or someone else in your office may have already assembled similar slides in a different presentation. Tap into those presentations to save time. You can go grab a slide, a series of slides, or an entire presentation and insert it into your new presentation. Again, don't reinvent the wheel! Use the Reuse Slides feature in PowerPoint.

If the slides that you want to duplicate are in another presentation, insert them by browsing out to that location.

Within your existing presentation, select *New Slide* and *Reuse Slides*.

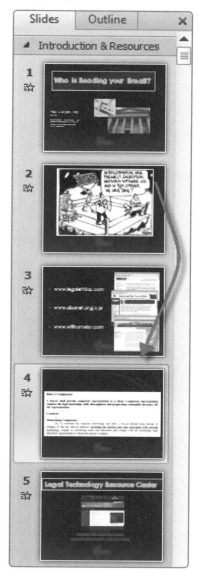

Figure 3.9 Dragging and Dropping an Inserted Slide

Figure 3.10 Reusing Slides in a Presentation

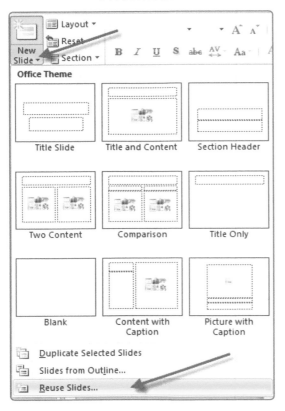

Select ***Browse*** (see Figure 3.11) and find the presentation that has the slides you would like to reuse. Open the file that has the desired slides.

Figure 3.11 Browse for Previous Presentations

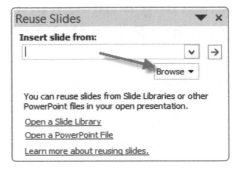

Once you open the file, the slides will load and can be viewed in a task pane on the right side of the screen. At this point, you have a couple of options, both of which are shown in Figure 3.12:

- You can right-click to insert one slide or all slides.
- You may also want to check the box labeled ***Keep source formatting*** to preserve the formatting from the original presentation. This will prevent the inserted slide from adopting the destination theme.

Figure 3.12 Options for Adding Existing Slides to a New Presentation

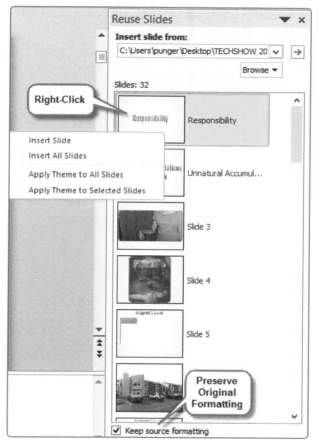

Deleting a Slide

Deleting slides is an essential function within the program. As with all other Microsoft Office applications, there are multiple ways to accomplish this function.

To delete a single slide in PowerPoint, simply right-click on the slide and select ***Delete Slide*** (see Figure 3.13). You may also left-click on the slide and hit the Delete key on the keyboard.

Figure 3.13 Deleting a Slide

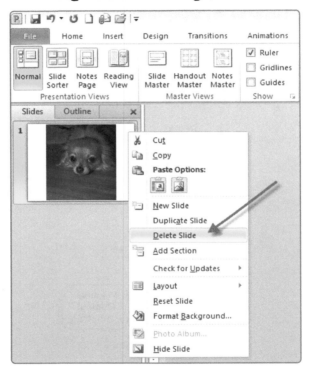

Deleting Multiple Slides

Hold down the ***Ctrl*** key on your keyboard and left-click on all the slides you want to delete. Then right-click on any of the selected slides and select ***Delete Slides*** or hit the ***Delete*** key on the keyboard.

Hiding Slides

Sometimes you do not want to delete a slide, but you do not want it to show in a presentation. This happens frequently in opening statements when you have created a series of slides about a particular topic, but at the last minute you or the judge decides it is not appropriate to introduce that subject matter in the opening.

Deleting the slide has a couple of bad consequences. First, and the most obvious, you may want to show the slide later, and by deleting it, it will be gone unless you have a backup. Second, you may mess up the slide numbering that you have depended on. For instance, if you had printed your slides with numbers or you have committed a few slide numbers to memory so you can jump around in your presenting, deleting any slides will completely throw off your numbering.

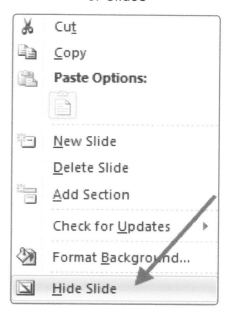

Figure 3.14 Hiding a Slide or Slides

To hide a slide or series of slides, hold down the **Ctrl** key on your keyboard and left-click on all the slides you want to hide. Then right-click on any of the selected slides and select **Hide Slide** (see Figure 3.14).

Cut, Copy, and Paste

Use Cut, Copy, and Paste when you need to move or copy whole slides, or text or objects within a slide, to a different location. For example, if you have a picture in one slide that you would like to paste into another slide, select the picture and click *Copy* in the **Home** ribbon (shown in Figure 3.15). This will copy the image into the Windows clipboard. The clipboard will store twenty-four items.

Figure 3.15 Copying in PowerPoint

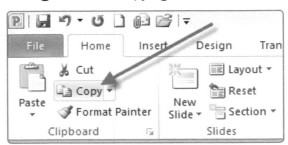

Then reposition the cursor in the location where you would like to paste the picture and select *Paste* from the **Home** ribbon.

The following are some helpful keyboard shortcuts for cutting, pasting, and copying:

Task	Keystroke
Cut	Ctrl+X
Copy	Ctrl+C
Paste	Crtl+V
Undo	Ctrl+Z
Redo	Ctrl+Y

To Paste from the Twenty-Four-Item Clipboard Menu

A little-known or forgotten feature of all Microsoft Office applications is that the clipboard can actually hold up to twenty-four items. Many people think that the clipboard holds only the last item copied.

To activate the clipboard, select the launcher from the Clipboard group in the **Home** ribbon as shown in Figure 3.16.

Now you are ready to copy items into the clipboard. As you select and copy text or objects, they will appear in the clipboard. In other words, PowerPoint will display a list of all items currently available in the clipboard.

To paste an item into your slide, position the cursor in the desired location within your slide show and left-click on the item you want to paste. To clear the clipboard completely, select **Clear All** (see Figure 3.16). To clear one item from the clipboard, right-click on it and select **Delete**.

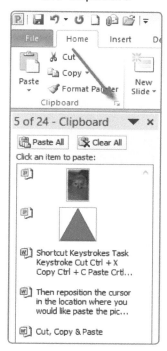

Figure 3.16 Activating the Clipboard

Creating a Title Slide

Some of PowerPoint's standard design schemes are very good. However, they tend to be overused and have distractions that can interfere with pictures, legal graphics, video, and documents that are used quite frequently in legal presentations. For this reason, it is a good idea to create your own design. It is very easy to create a professional-looking title slide on your own.

1. Open PowerPoint and start with a brand-new presentation. **Ctrl+N** will also create a new slide show.

2. Right-click on the background if you would like to change the color. Select ***Format Background*** (see Figure 4.1) and choose the desired color or gradient fill, or insert a graphic.

3. From the **Home** ribbon, change the font, font color, and size to the desired appearance. For example, in Figure 4.2, the font is Tw Cen MT (Twentieth Century Monotype), its color is dark blue, and the size is 32 points.

Figure 4.1 Formatting the Background

Figure 4.2 Formatting the Font

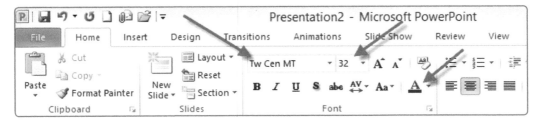

Figure 4.3 Reflection Text Effect

4. To create a text effect, such as the reflection font seen in the phrase "Plaintiff's Opening Statement" in Figure 4.3 above, place your cursor anywhere inside the text, and from the contextual **Format** ribbon, select *Text Effects* (see Figure 4.4) and *Reflection* (see Figure 4.5).

Figure 4.4 Adding Text Effects

Figure 4.5 Reflection Text Effect

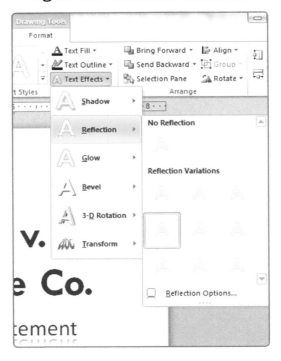

5. You may want to save your hard work and reuse this format and color scheme in a later presentation. To do this, you can save your presentation as a theme. Learn about saving themes, master slides, and templates in Lesson 25.

Inserting Custom Graphic as Background

Inserting Picture or Custom Graphic as Background

You may want to insert a photograph or a custom graphic that a graphic designer creates for your presentation or your law office. Many backgrounds can be downloaded free from Microsoft (office.microsoft.com),

or you can buy them from vendors like Digital Juice (www.digitaljuice.com). These backgrounds will be saved as graphic files, most often in JPG or PNG format. Figure 5.1 shows an example of a custom background created by a graphic designer. It was saved as "Affinity.JPG."

Figure 5.1 Custom Background

This section explains how to load a graphic file so it becomes the background for your slides.

1. Save and note the location where you save your custom background file.

2. Right-click on an open area within your PowerPoint slide and select *Format Background*. Select the *Fill* category in the left panel, choose the radio button *Picture or texture fill*, and then click *File* (see Figure 5.2).

Figure 5.2 Formatting a Background

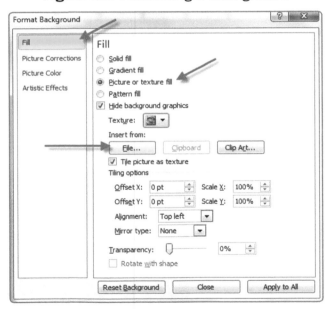

3. Browse to find the image file and double-click to select it. If you want to apply that backdrop to just the one slide, click *Close*. If you want to apply the backdrop to all slides, click *Apply to All*.

Animated Bullet Points

Creating Bullet Point Lists

As indicated previously, bullet points can be effective if used sparingly and in the form of short sentences or headlines. Minimize the amount of text as much as possible. Studies show that people can remember as much as 28 percent more *without* the use of bullet points when those bullet point slides contain too much information for the audience to absorb while trying to read the slide and listen to the presenter. Also remember to *not* over-animate. Be conservative. If the animation is a distraction, you are not making your point. If you are presenting in the courtroom, I recommend a basic animation like fade, appear, or wipe.

1. On the **Home** ribbon, click *New Slide* (see Figure 6.1). Select *Title and Content*.

2. Now click in the *Click to add title* area and add some text as the heading for the list.

3. Click in the bulleted *Click to add text* field and add the first of your bullet points. Hit *Enter* to advance to the next line and add additional bullets.

Figure 6.1 New Slide

4. To change the appearance of the bullets in the list, select the existing bullet list. From the **Home** ribbon, click on the drop-down
   menu from the bullet-point toolbar button (see Figure 6.2) and
   double-click to select the desired bullet style.

Figure 6.2 Drop-Down Menu on Bullet-Point Toolbar

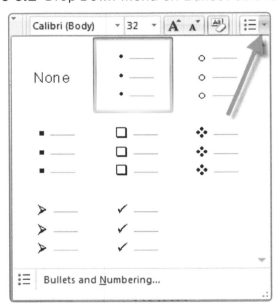

5. To animate your bulleted list so each item comes in one at a time,
   select the **Animations** ribbon and then **Add Animation** (see Figure
   6.3). In the gallery, select the desired effect to apply. I recommend
   applying the animation to the first bullet point; then, as you com-
   plete your bullet point, the animation effect will carry over to the
   next bullet point as you hit **Enter** and type the text.

Figure 6.3 Animation Ribbon

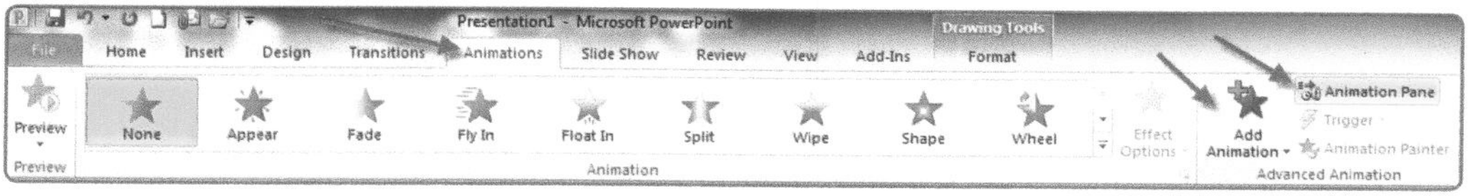

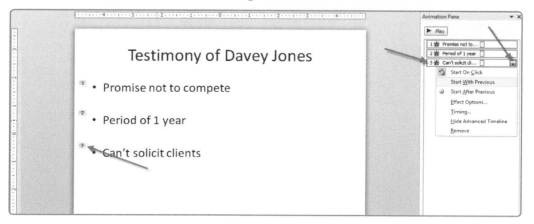

6. Choosing ***Animation Pane*** (see Figure 6.3) will allow you to customize the options and properties of the effect that you apply. If you click on ***Animation Pane***, a task pane will appear on the far right-hand side of the screen. Select the desired bullet points to animate, as shown in Figure 6.4 below. Click on the drop-down menu to change when the bullet should appear (on a click, with previous, after previous) and choose other options (dimming, timing, with sound, etc.).

Figure 6.4 Customizing Animation for Bullet Points

Inserting Clip Art

Clip art refers to premade artwork, images, or illustrations that can be added to presentations. Clip art can enhance slides at appropriate times, but please use it conservatively! It can make a presentation look unprofessional if the images appear cheesy or cartoonish. If in doubt, get some colleagues' opinions or don't use it. Always ask yourself, "Does this graphic or clip art 'advance the ball'? Does it add value to my message or presentation?"

Clip art is used extensively in all sorts of projects, ranging from homemade greeting cards and desktop publishing to commercial presentations and products. Clip art for PowerPoint is in electronic format and found in a clip art gallery along with some stock photography. The clip art from the gallery within PowerPoint is licensed to you. According to the Microsoft Services Agreement, it becomes your content. Microsoft does not claim ownership. See http://windows.microsoft.com/en-us/windows-live/microsoft-services-agreement.

1. To insert clip art, from the **Insert** ribbon, select ***Clip Art*** (see Figure 7.1).

Figure 7.1 Clip Art on Insert Ribbon

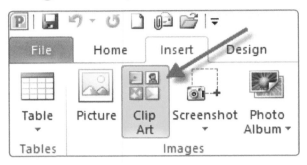

2. Define your search. In the example in Figure 7.2, we are searching for a gavel.

Figure 7.2 Searching for Clip Art

3. PowerPoint will return a list of results. Hover over the image you want to use, and a drop-down menu will appear (see Figure 7.2). Select *Insert*.

4. To resize clip art, always use one of the four corner handles, as shown in Figure 7.3. Otherwise, the image will lose its dimensions.

Figure 7.3 Handles Used to Resize Clip Art

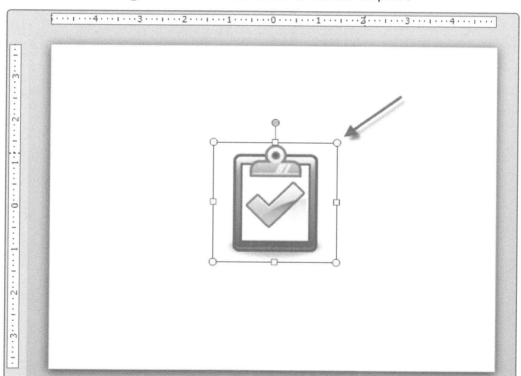

Inserting and Working with Photographs

Inserting photographs in PowerPoint slides is essential to many presentations. Often people insert photographs to make slides look more attractive, but it is highly likely that you will use photos to deliver important information that words alone cannot convey; for example, evidence in trial, introduction of people or players, and, most frequently, displaying documents. Collectively, these pictures or graphics are referred to in PowerPoint as **Pictures**.

Inserting Photographs

To insert a photograph, create a new slide or select an existing slide, select the ***Insert*** ribbon and click on ***Picture*** (see Figure 8.1). Browse to the location where the photograph is saved. You can either double-click on the file or select it and click ***Open*** at the bottom of the dialog box.

Figure 8.1 Inserting a Photograph

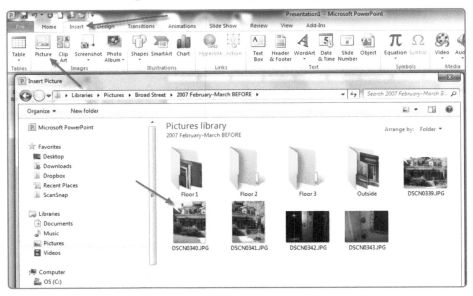

Changing Your Background Slide Color to Black

Often it is desirable to make the background color a solid black when displaying photographs or clip art. This will eliminate any distracting graphics from your slide backdrop. It also makes inconsistent photograph sizes less noticeable between slides.

Figure 8.2 Format Background

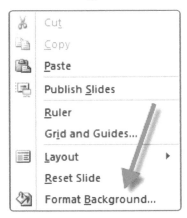

1. Right-click on the background and select ***Format Background*** (see Figure 8.2).

2. Select the desired color and click ***Close*** to apply the color to just that slide (see Figure 8.3).

Figure 8.3 Applying Color to Background

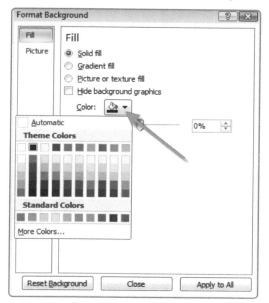

Resizing Photographs

PowerPoint often will insert a picture in a size that doesn't fit in a way that you anticipated. Depending upon the resolution of the picture, it may be too small or too large. Inserted pictures can be easily resized by using the same method as resizing clip art images. Use your mouse to click and drag the resizing handles (see Figure 8.4). *Always use the corners to resize an image* so you do not skew the image. The entire picture can also be moved by clicking and dragging the image itself to another location on the slide.

Figure 8.4 Resizing Handles on a Photograph

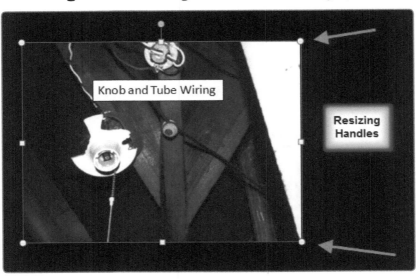

Adjusting the Quality of Photographs

You can adjust the quality of a photograph by clicking on the photo to activate the **Picture Tools/Format** contextual ribbon. You will see a group called **Adjust** on the far left-hand side of the ribbon, which is shown in Figure 8.5 below. Here you can adjust the photo's brightness, contrast, and color. You can also decrease the size of your PowerPoint file by using **Compress Pictures**.

Figure 8.5 Adjustments on the Picture Tools/Format Ribbon

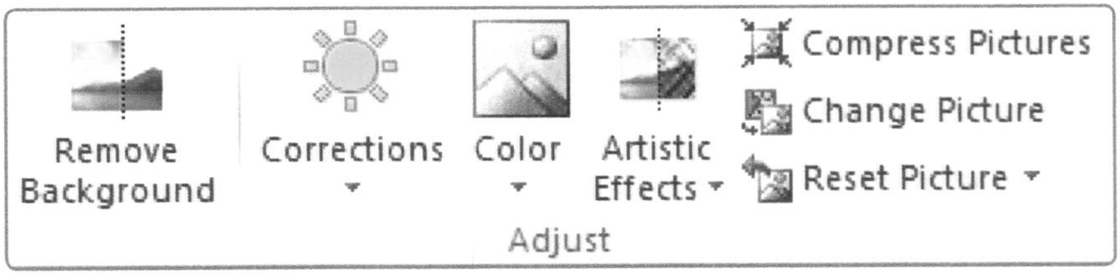

Reducing File Size by Compressing Pictures

Photographs can sometimes be very large files, thereby inflating the file size of your PowerPoint presentation. This can slow down PowerPoint's performance and, in some cases, can make the presentation unstable. Instability is the last thing you need in the middle of a presentation.

Most photographs do not need to be high resolution to be used with PowerPoint and a projector. Using PowerPoint's Compress Pictures feature, you can reduce the size of a PowerPoint file, optimizing stability and performance.

1. Double-click on a photo to reveal the **Picture Tools/Format** contextual ribbon, shown in Figure 8.6 below.

Figure 8.6 Compress Pictures Feature on Picture Tools/Format Ribbon

2. Click on **Compress Pictures** (see Figure 8.6 above). The dialog box shown in Figure 8.7 will appear.

   - Select **Apply only to this picture** if you do not want all photographs in the presentation to be compressed.

   - Select **Delete cropped areas of pictures** if you want to delete cropped areas of photographs.

   - Select **Print (220 ppi)** to compress photographs, yet still maintain quality images.

Figure 8.7 Compress Pictures Dialog Box

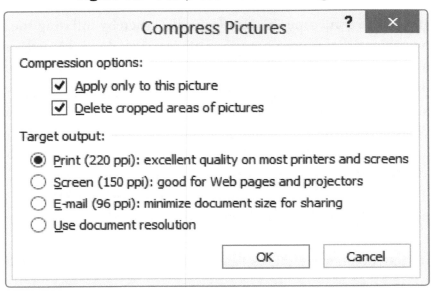

Inserting Multiple Photographs at Once

Many times you will need to insert multiple photographs into a Power-Point slide show. Inserting one at a time can be very tedious, requiring that you resize each photo on every single slide, repeating the process for every photo that you wish to insert. By using the **Photo Album** function, you can insert all photographs at one time. This is especially helpful if you have dozens of photographs, but it can still save you time and aggravation even if you have only a few photos.

1. Open PowerPoint and select *Photo Album* from the **Insert** ribbon, as shown in Figure 9.1.

Figure 9.1 Photo Album on Insert Ribbon

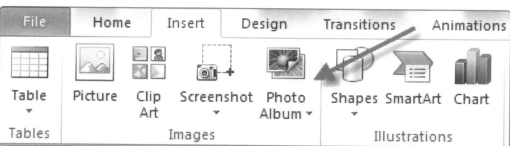

2. Click the ***File/Disk*** button and then browse to the location of your digital photographs (see Figure 9.2 below). Select the desired photographs (*Tip:* **CTRL+A** will select all) and click ***Insert***.

Figure 9.2 Selecting Photos in Photo Album

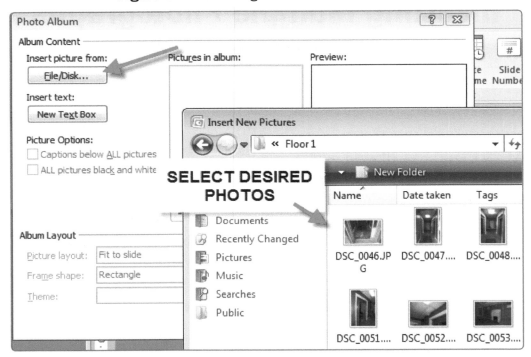

3. You can reorder the photos, rotate them, and adjust brightness and contrast, all within the Photo Album dialog box (see Figure 9.3). Think of it as a control panel. Select ***Fit to slide*** as the picture layout in the Album Layout section and then click ***Create*** to create the presentation. This will make a brand new file, as opposed to inserting the photos into an existing file.

Figure 9.3 Photo Album Dialog Box

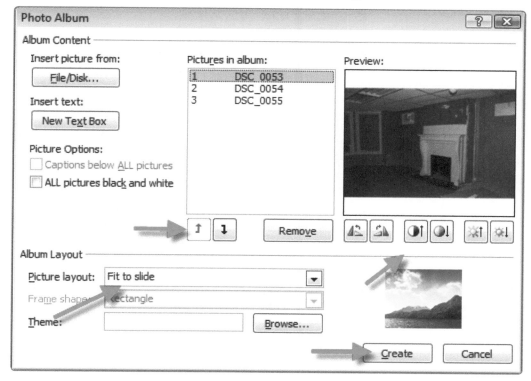

4. If you want to use these slides within a different already existing PowerPoint presentation, save this file (be sure to note the location) and exit. Open the other PowerPoint file, and from the **Home** ribbon, select *New Slide* and *Reuse Slides*. Browse out to the presentation that you just created and insert all or just the desired slides.

Inserting a PDF into PowerPoint

Many documents and graphics today are saved as PDFs. However, inserting an image saved as a PDF (Portable Document Format) is unfortunately *not* an option from within PowerPoint. A PDF is not a true graphic file.

You can convert the PDF to a JPG or TIFF file by opening it in Adobe Acrobat Standard or Pro (the free Reader does not give you that option) and selecting ***File > Save As Other > Image***. Then choose the desired format and convert the PDF. This will give you the highest resolution and best result. The steps are shown below in Figure 10.1.

Figure 10.1 Converting a PDF for Use in PowerPoint

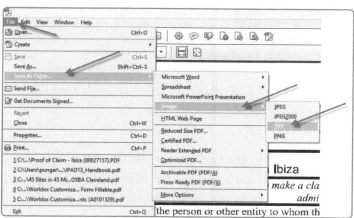

> **TIP**
>
> There are a couple of tricks you can use to quickly insert images from PDFs directly into PowerPoint.

Open a PDF file. Zoom in or out on the document. Line up the PDF perfectly on the screen so you can see everything needed.

1. In PowerPoint, go to the **Insert** ribbon and click *Screenshot*, as shown in Figure 10.2.

Figure 10.2 Screenshot Function on Insert Ribbon

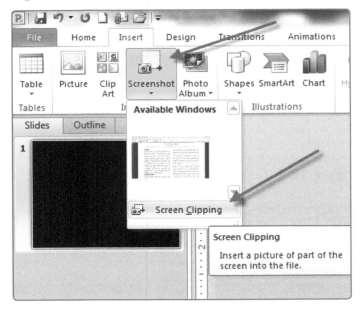

2. The PDF you have open will show in the Available Windows box. It will appear washed out. Using the *Screen Clipping* tool (see Figure 10.2 above), left-click and drag to select the area of the PDF you

want to insert in your slide. When you release the mouse button, PowerPoint will place the clip into your PowerPoint slide, as shown in Figure 10.3.

Figure 10.3 Clip from PDF Inserted into PowerPoint Slide

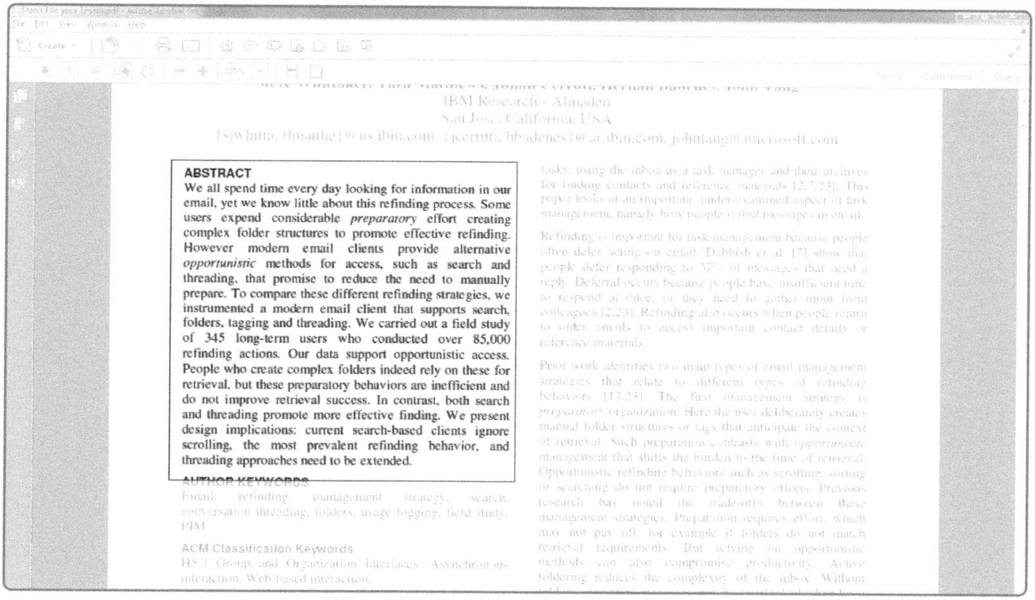

Using Windows Vista, Windows 7, or Windows 8 Snipping Tool

If you do not have PowerPoint 2010, you can always use the integrated Windows Snipping Tool to capture any object on your screen and then insert the image into PowerPoint.

1. Open anything that you want to capture on the screen. It could be something in a PDF or a Word document or even on a website. Line up the image perfectly on the screen so you can see everything needed.

2. Launch the ***Snipping Tool***. The Snipping Tool is part of the Windows Operating System that is available in Windows Vista or later. The easiest way to find and launch the Snipping Tool is by hitting the Windows button on your keyboard and type the word "Snipping". (see Figure 10.4). Then left-click to launch.

Figure 10.4 Windows Snipping Tool Icon

3. Click ***New*** and then choose one of the snipping options, such as ***Rectangular Snip*** (see Figure 10.5). Select the area of the document or image to snip by left-clicking and dragging your mouse.

Figure 10.5 Snipping Options

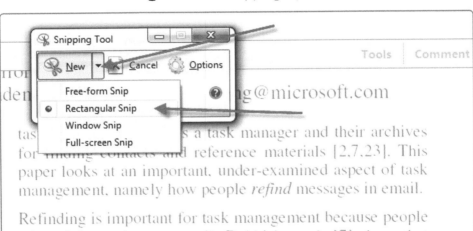

4. When you release the mouse button, your snip will appear and you can click *Copy* (see Figure 10.6) to place it in your Windows clipboard. Switch to PowerPoint and paste the clip into your PowerPoint slide. Also note in Figure 10.6 the annotation tools and the options to save or e-mail the clip.

Figure 10.6 Copy Function in Snipping Tool

The Snipping Tool is good for many general office uses as well:

- grabbing an excerpt of a paragraph within a contract to quote in a letter
- grabbing an excerpt from a deposition to quote in a letter or a witness outline
- capturing a photo (or part of a photo) to insert in your document

TIP

I recommend adding the Snipping Tool to your Quick Launch bar in Windows. It makes it much easier to grab screenshots on the fly.

Text Boxes

For lawyers, labels are essential to many photographs and documents. For example, we need labels to explain photographic evidence, describe a process, or mark something with an exhibit number. Text boxes are used to create these labels.

Inserting Labels and Captions Using Text Boxes

1. Click on the *Insert* ribbon and then select *Text Box*, as shown in Figure 11.1.

Figure 11.1 Text Box Function on Insert Ribbon

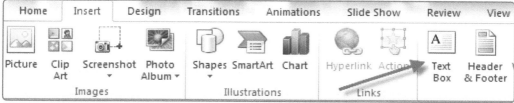

2. Move your cursor to where you want to place the text box and left-click.

3. Type the desired text and format it appropriately (i.e., color, font, and size).

4. To format the text box, right-click on it and use the **_Format Shape_** dialog box that appears (see Figure 11.2). For example, to create a white background, select **_Fill_**, then **_Solid fill_**, and then the fill color white.

Figure 11.2 Format Shape Dialog Box

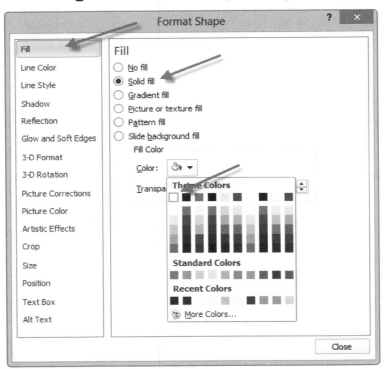

5. Finally, using your mouse, drag the box (like any other object) to its final location on the slide. An example is shown in Figure 11.3 below.

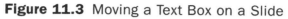

Figure 11.3 Moving a Text Box on a Slide

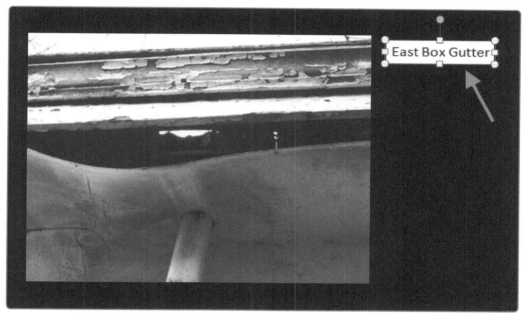

Inserting Shapes and Lines

Inserting a Rectangle, Circle, Arrow, or Line

You may want to draw an object that has a specific shape on a slide to describe a process or, many times, create a rectangle or circle to draw attention to an area on a photograph.

1. On the **Insert** ribbon, click ***Shapes***, and then select the desired shape. In Figure 12.1 below, the choice is a rectangle.

Figure 12.1 Choosing a Shape

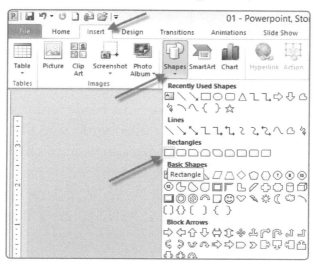

2. Draw the shape by left-clicking and dragging anywhere on the slide. Release the mouse button when you have the desired size. A rectangle has been drawn in Figure 12.2. You can resize the rectangle by selecting the re-sizing handle (similar to resizing a photograph in Lesson 8).

Figure 12.2 Rectangle Drawn in a Photo

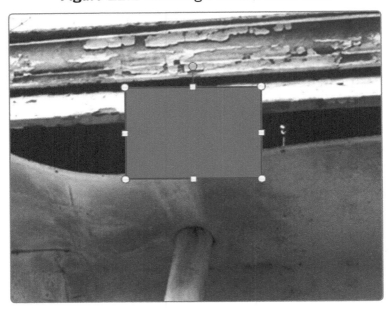

3. You will probably want to change the border color and fill color. In Figure 12.2, the rectangle has a blue border and fill color. We want a red border with no fill color. We also want to change the thickness of the border line.

4. To change the fill color and border, right-click on the newly created object and select **_Format Shape_**. A dialog box will appear as shown in the figures below.

5. Select ***Fill*** and then ***No fill***, as shown in Figure 12.3.

Figure 12.3 Changing the Fill Color

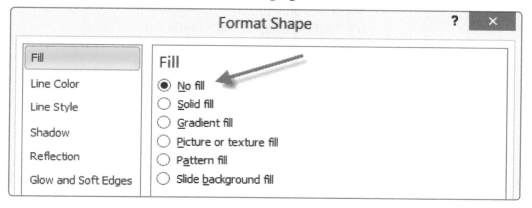

6. Select ***Line Color***, ***Solid line***, and then the desired color. In the example in Figure 12.4, the color choice is red.

Figure 12.4 Changing the Line Color

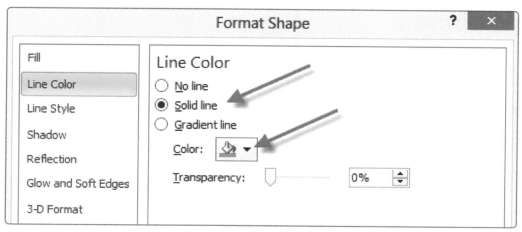

7. Select **Line Style**. In the Width box, use the arrows or enter a number to make the border thicker or thinner. In Figure 12.5, the width is being changed to 4 pt.

Figure 12.5 Changing the Line Width

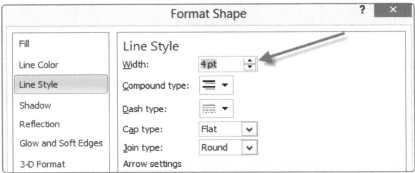

8. To animate the rectangle (or any other shape) so it appears that it is being drawn on the screen with a mouse-click, select the rectangle and then on the **Animations** ribbon select **Add Animation**. Under the Entrance category, select **Wheel**. The steps are shown in Figure 12.6 below.

Figure 12.6 Adding Animation to a Shape

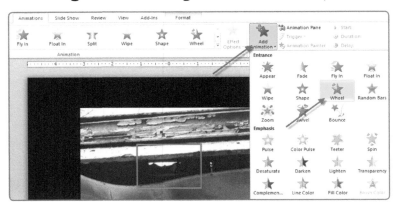

Using Color and Animation to Fill Objects

Filling an object with color and adding motion can be extremely useful to give the appearance of an actual animation. You can use this technique to demonstrate hundreds of things. Some examples include the following:

- highlighting a portion of a document
- blood flow
- a clot or plaque traveling through an artery
- formation of ice
- rain or movement of water
- pathway of smoke or air
- applying a solid or semitransparent color to a diagram or illustration

Adding Color and Animation to Show Blood Movement

In this example, we are going to give the illusion that blood is flowing through a vessel. It requires that we first have two images: (1) a picture/graphic of a blood vessel, and (2) a picture/graphic of blood. Both can be obtained through a licensed or license-free source of stock photography or graphics.

1. Select a plain dark background free of any graphics (black is preferable).

2. From the **Insert** ribbon, select *Picture*. Browse to the graphic of the blood vessel and double-click to insert it into the PowerPoint slide. The inserted picture is shown in Figure 13.1.

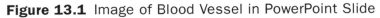

Figure 13.1 Image of Blood Vessel in PowerPoint Slide

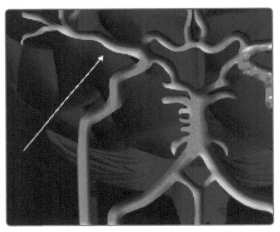

3. From the **Insert** ribbon, click on *Shapes*. Then select the *Scribble* tool, which is shown in Figure 13.2.

Figure 13.2 Scribble Tool

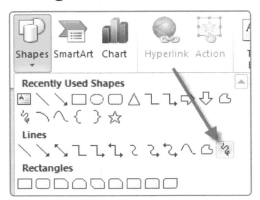

4. Using the pencil pointer, trace the edges of the blood vessel to draw a shape, as shown in Figure 13.3.

5. Right-click on the drawn shape and select *Format Picture*. In the dialog box, choose *Fill* and *Picture or texture fill*, and then click *File* to browse to your blood graphic. Double-click to insert the blood graphic as a fill color for the blood vessel. Go back to the left side of the box, select *Line Color*, and then choose *No Line*. Finally, click on *Close*. Most of these steps are shown in Figure 13.4 below.

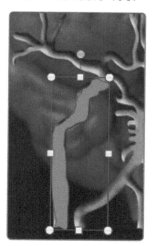

Figure 13.3 Shape Drawn on an Image with Scribble Tool

Figure 13.4 Adding a Blood Graphic to a Blood Vessel Image

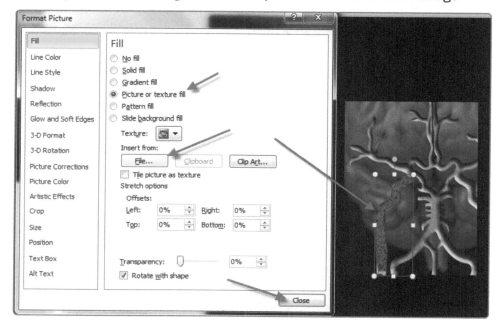

6. Animate the blood graphic by selecting the hand-drawn shape. On the **Animations** ribbon, click *Wipe*. Under **Effect Options**, select *From Bottom* to show the blood (in this example) traveling upward. These steps are shown in Figure 13.5.

Figure 13.5 Animating a Blood Graphic

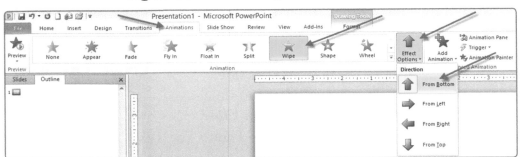

7. To change the speed of the blood flow, click the *Animation Pane* on the **Animations** Ribbon (to the far right on Figure 13.5 above). On the task pane, right-click on the animation and select *Effect Options* (see Figure 13.6).

8. Under the **Timing** tab, select the desired speed using the *Duration* drop-down menu. Duration options are shown in Figure 13.7, with 3 seconds chosen.

Figure 13.6 Changing an Animation Effect

Figure 13.7 Setting the Timing on an Animation

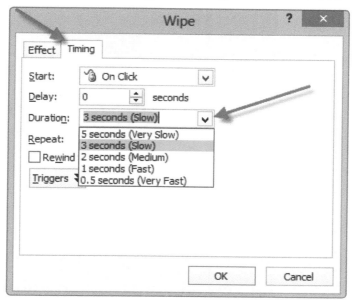

Adding Color and Animation to Fill an Object, Graphic, or Photo

In this example, we are going to use color to fill in part of a graphic of the human brain. We want to highlight different parts of the brain so a presenter can educate an audience (or a jury) about the function of a specific section of the brain or any damage that has been done to it.

1. Insert a graphic file into your slide (***Insert > Picture***).

2. From the **Insert** ribbon, select ***Shapes > Lines > Free Form***.

3. Use your mouse to draw the area that you want to fill with color. Left-click and hold to draw the desired shape. An example is shown in Figure 13.8.

Figure 13.8 Drawing a Shape on the Image of a Brain

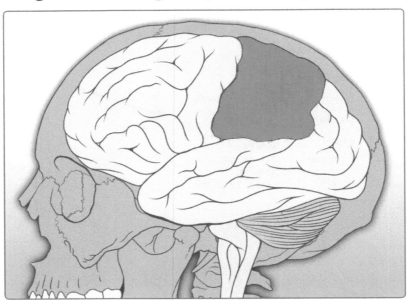

4. Right-click on the drawn shape and select ***Format Shape*** to get the dialog box shown in Figure 13.9.

   i. Set the color by clicking ***Fill***, then choosing ***Solid fill*** and the desired color. In Figure 13.9, the choice is red.

   ii. Adjust the transparency to between 40 and 60 percent to let the texture from the graphic behind the shape bleed through. Figure 13.9 shows a transparency of 50 percent.

Figure 13.10 shows the brain image with a shape that has the color and fill as specified in Step 4. Note that there is a white border, or line, around the shape.

Figure 13.9 Formatting a Shape's Fill and Transparency

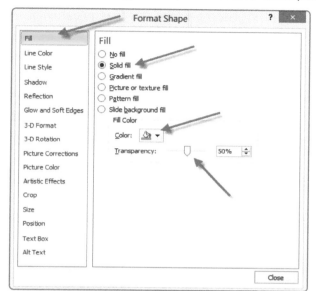

Figure 13.10 Image of Brain with Shape Drawn on One Section

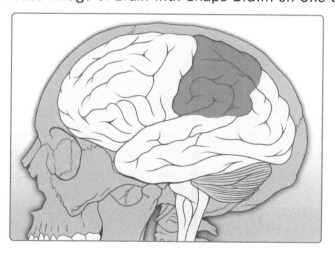

5. To format a line bordering a shape, select *Line Color* in the **Format Shape** dialog box. Then choose *No line* (as shown in Figure 13.11) or choose *Solid line* and pick a color. You can also adjust the thickness of the line by selecting *Line Style*.

Figure 13.11 Formatting a Shape's Line Border

6. To animate colored shapes or objects on an image, select the first shape that you would like to animate. On the **Animations** ribbon, select an option such as *Fade*, which has been chosen in Figure 13.12. Repeat for each area that you want to animate.

Figure 13.12 Animating a Colored Shape or Object

Document Callouts

Callouts are essential when displaying documents on PowerPoint slides. Text is simply too small to see on a slide when the full document is displayed to fit on the slide. Callouts give you an opportunity to show the full document first, which establishes credibility with a jury or your audience that you are indeed showing the full document and not hiding something. Then, using the callout technique, you can "blow up" or "call out" the relevant portion of a document to a size that everyone can read. Here is an example of how this would look in a presentation.

First show the entire document, as displayed in Figure 14.1:

Figure 14.1 Full Page of Document on PowerPoint Slide

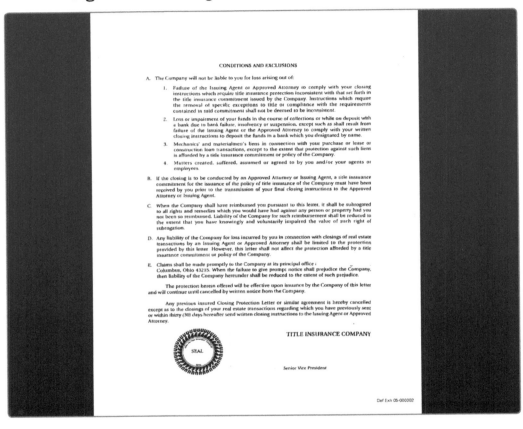

Second, draw attention to an area on the document. Figure 14.2 shows item B marked with a red rectangle.

Figure 14.2 Marking Specific Text

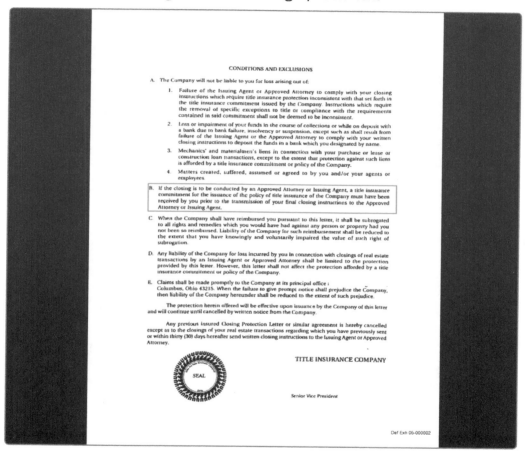

Finally, call out the paragraph that you need to display. In Figure 14.3, the text in the red rectangle has been enlarged and part of it is highlighted in yellow.

Figure 14.3 Callout of Specific Text

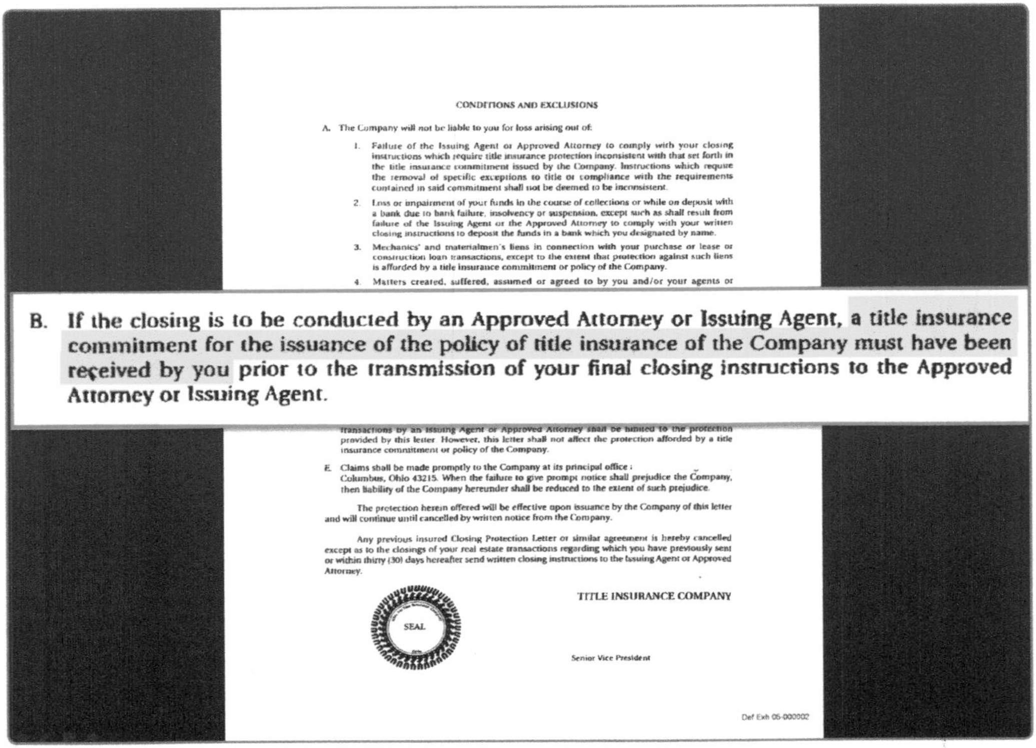

CONDITIONS AND EXCLUSIONS

A. The Company will not be liable to you for loss arising out of:

1. Failure of the Issuing Agent or Approved Attorney to comply with your closing instructions which require title insurance protection inconsistent with that set forth in the title insurance commitment issued by the Company. Instructions which require the removal of specific exceptions to title or compliance with the requirements contained in said commitment shall not be deemed to be inconsistent.
2. Loss or impairment of your funds in the course of collections or while on deposit with a bank due to bank failure, insolvency or suspension, except such as shall result from failure of the Issuing Agent or the Approved Attorney to comply with your written closing instructions to deposit the funds in a bank which you designated by name.
3. Mechanics' and materialmen's liens in connection with your purchase or lease or construction loan transactions, except to the extent that protection against such liens is afforded by a title insurance commitment or policy of the Company.
4. Matters created, suffered, assumed or agreed to by you and/or your agents or

B. If the closing is to be conducted by an Approved Attorney or Issuing Agent, a title insurance commitment for the issuance of the policy of title insurance of the Company must have been received by you prior to the transmission of your final closing instructions to the Approved Attorney or Issuing Agent.

transactions by an Issuing Agent or Approved Attorney shall be limited to the protection provided by this letter. However, this letter shall not affect the protection afforded by a title insurance commitment or policy of the Company.

E. Claims shall be made promptly to the Company at its principal office : Columbus, Ohio 43215. When the failure to give prompt notice shall prejudice the Company, then liability of the Company hereunder shall be reduced to the extent of such prejudice.

The protection herein offered will be effective upon issuance by the Company of this letter and will continue until cancelled by written notice from the Company.

Any previous insured Closing Protection Letter or similar agreement is hereby cancelled except as to the closings of your real estate transactions regarding which you have previously sent or within thirty (30) days hereafter send written closing instructions to the Issuing Agent or Approved Attorney.

SEAL

TITLE INSURANCE COMPANY

Senior Vice President

Def Exh 05-000002

Creating Document Callouts

1. Scan the document that you would like to use and save it as a TIFF or JPG file. Note the location where it is saved.
2. On the **Insert** ribbon, click ***Picture***. Browse to the location where the TIFF or JPG is saved. You can either double-click on the file or select it and click ***Open*** at the bottom of the dialog box.

3. The document will appear. Resize it so it fits on the page.

4. To draw attention to part of the document, insert a rectangle shape (***Insert > Shapes***). Format the shape so it has no fill, and change the line color to something that will stand out, like red or black (right-click on the shape and select ***Format Shape***). Finally, animate the shape—using a fade effect, for example. (See Lesson 12, "Inserting Shapes and Lines," to review this process.)

5. Now duplicate the document by right-clicking on it and selecting ***Copy*** and then ***Paste*** to place the copy next to the original. Now there are two of the same documents on the slide, as shown in Figure 14.4.

Figure 14.4 Document and Copy

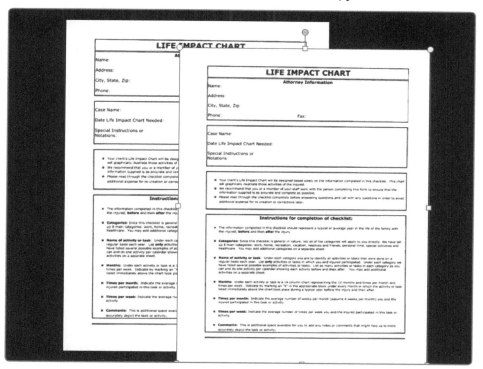

6. Click on one of the images to get the cropping tool to appear on the contextual **Picture Tools/Format** ribbon (see Figure 14.5). Create the callout by using the Crop tool on the copied document.

Figure 14.5 Crop Tool

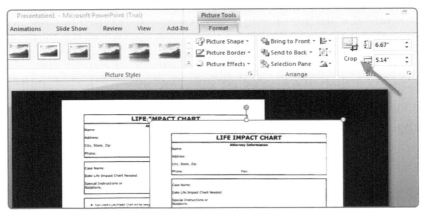

7. Drag the Crop handles (see Figure 14.6) to remove the portions of the document that you do not want to show. When you are finished cropping, left-click in any open area of the slide.

Figure 14.6 Crop Handles

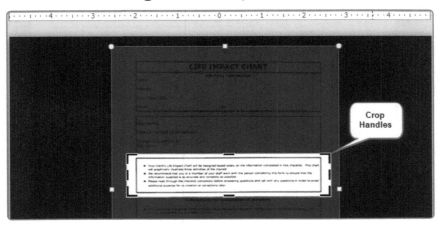

8. After you have created the callout, resize it using the corner handles (see Figure 14.7). Move the callout to a good position on the page, typically the middle or top-middle of the slide.

Figure 14.7 Corner Handles

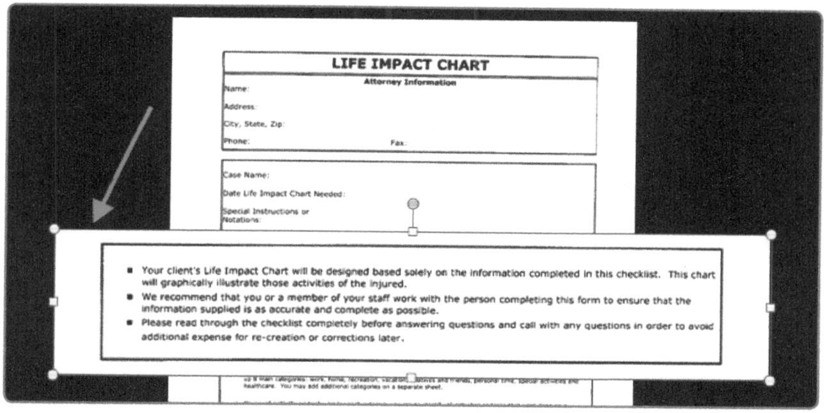

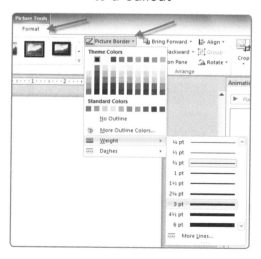

9. Add a border around the callout by selecting ***Picture Border*** from the **Picture Tools/Format** ribbon. Select the desired border color and weight. These steps are shown in Figure 14.8.

10. You can animate the callout from the **Animations** ribbon. With the callout selected, click ***Add Animation*** and choose an entrance effect for the callout, like **Zoom**, as shown in Figure 14.9.

Figure 14.8 Adding a Border to a Callout

Figure 14.9 Animation for Callout

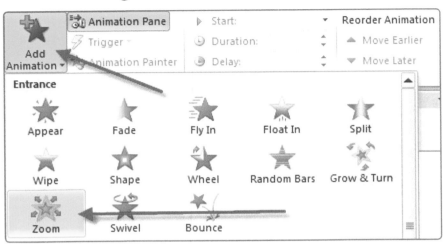

11. To add highlighting to the callout, I recommend using another program like Photoshop Elements, but you can do it (with mediocre results) within PowerPoint. Select ***Shapes*** on the **Insert** ribbon and draw a rectangular box around the text (see Figure 14.10).

Figure 14.10 Drawing a Rectangle around a Callout for Highlighting

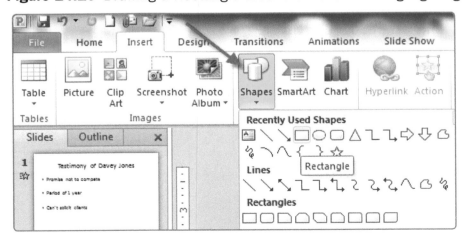

12. Right-click on the new rectangle and select *Format Shape*. Remove the border by selecting *Line Color* in the dialog box and then *No Line*.

13. While you are still in the dialog box, select *Fill* and *Solid fill*. Apply a yellow or green fill color. Use the Transparency slider to adjust the setting from the default 0 percent to somewhere between 40 and 60 percent. Figure 14.11 shows these steps and the resulting highlight.

Figure 14.11 Adding Yellow Highlight to Callout

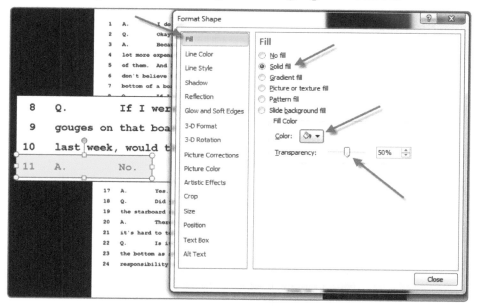

Alternative Highlighting Methods for Documents

To achieve high-quality highlighting, it is best to bring the callout into a photo-editing program like Adobe Photoshop or Adobe Photoshop Elements, perform the crop and highlighting in one of those programs, and then save the file as a separate JPG to be inserted. This takes significantly longer than the above procedure, but it provides an excellent result.

A lesser alternative, but certainly an OK work-around to purchasing a program like Photoshop or Photoshop Elements is using the Snipping Tool that is part of the Windows operating system. (This tool was discussed in Lesson 10, "Inserting a PDF into PowerPoint.")

Other Alternatives

- If working with a text-searchable PDF, apply the highlighting in Adobe Acrobat and then use the Snipping Tool in Windows, or ***Insert > Screenshot*** in PowerPoint 2010 (See Lesson 10, "Inserting a PDF into PowerPoint," to review this process).

- If you have Sanction or TrialDirector, you could apply highlighting in Presentation Mode and then save the image. Browse to the saved location and then insert the file into PowerPoint.

- When you are within a slide show in PowerPoint, you can use the presentation annotation tools located in the lower left-hand corner (see Figure 14.12) and apply the highlighting.

Figure 14.12 Annotation Tools Highlighter

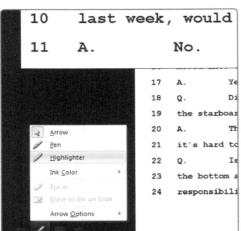

When you exit the presentation (by hitting *Escape*), select *Keep* in the dialog box (shown in Figure 14.13) to save your ink annotations.

Figure 14.13 Ink Annotations Dialog Box

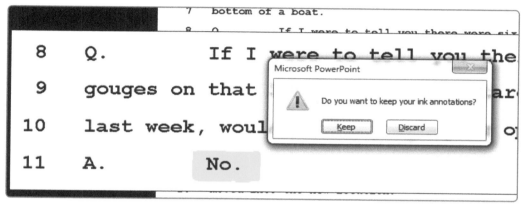

The "Ken Burns" Effect

Panning and Zooming on a Photograph or Document

The Ken Burns effect in PowerPoint is a technique where you pan and zoom on a photograph or document. It achieves a result similar to doing a callout (discussed in Lesson 14), but it doesn't involve creating a second image, and the animation is completely different. It is named for the American documentarian Ken Burns, who uses a similar effect in his films. The technique existed before he used it but has become associated with him because he made it popular.

Burns uses the effect in historical documentaries where, like in the courtroom or in many PowerPoint presentations, film or video-recorded material would be more effective to tell parts of the story. Movement is given to still photographs by gradually zooming in on subjects of interest and panning from one subject to another. For example, in a document like the one we see in Figure 15.1, one might slowly pan across the document and come to a rest on a single paragraph or area of the document.

Figure 15.1 Example of Ken Burns Effect

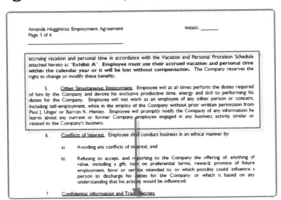

accruing vacation and personal time in accordance with the Vacation and Personal Proration Schedule attached hereto as "**Exhibit A**". **Employee must use their accrued vacation and personal time within the calendar year or it will be lost without compensation.** The Company reserves the right to change or modify these benefits.

   5.   Other Simultaneous Employment. Employee will at all times perform the duties required of him by the Company and devote his exclusive productive time, energy and skill to performing his duties for the Company. Employee will not work as an employee of any other person or concern, including self-employment, while in the employ of the Company without prior written permission from Paul J. Unger or Barron K. Henley. Employee will promptly notify the Company of any information he learns about any current or former Company employee engaged in any business activity similar or related to the Company's business.

The following are the steps to using this technique in a PowerPoint presentation.

1. Insert a photograph (or document) in your PowerPoint slide (***Insert > Picture***).

2. Select the photograph. On the **Animation** ribbon, select ***Add Animation*** and then ***Grow/Shrink***, as shown in Figure 15.2.

Figure 15.2 Grow/Shrink Feature

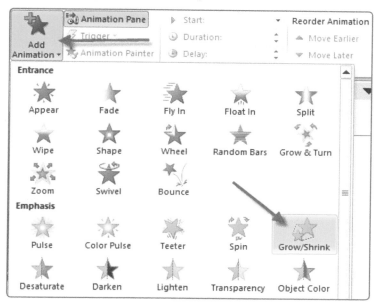

3. Select the ***Animation Pane***. Then right-click on the animation and select ***Timing*** (see Figure 15.3).

4. Under the **Timing** tab in the Grow/Shrink dialog box that appears, modify the duration to slow. This step is shown in Figure 15.4.

Figure 15.3 Animation Timing

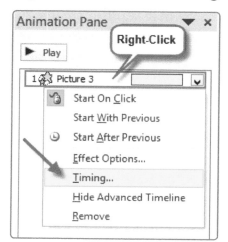

Figure 15.4 Modify Duration

5. Under the **Effect** tab, you may want to change the default from *Larger* to something smaller or bigger (shown in Figure 15.8). This will take a bit of trial, error, and testing to get the desired result.

6. With the photo still selected, click *Add Animation* and in the **Motion Paths** group, select *Custom Path* (shown in Figure 15.5).

Figure 15.5 Custom Motion Path

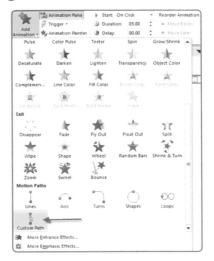

7. Using your mouse, left-click and draw a short line in the middle of the slide (see Figure 15.6). Click *Escape* to terminate the line.

8. With the animation selected in the **Animation Pane**, change the *Start* field to "With Previous." This step is shown in Figure 15.7.

9. Move the green and red arrows (see Figure 15.6) and keep testing until you have the desired zoom. This can be a bit tricky to get right. Use the *Play* button in the **Animation Pane** (see Figure 15.7) to test.

10. To tweak the zoom, right-click on the *Grow/Shrink* animation in the **Animation Pane** (first on the drop-down list in Figure 15.7). In the Grow/Shrink dialog box, under the **Effect** tab, modify the size by entering a custom value, as shown in Figure 15.8.

Figure 15.6 Drawing Line with Custom Path Tool

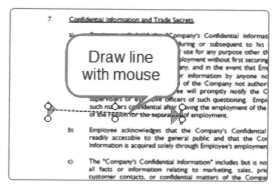

Figure 15.7 Change Start to "With Previous"

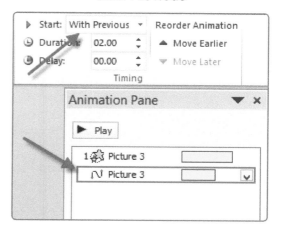

Figure 15.8 Adjusting the Zoom Using Custom Value

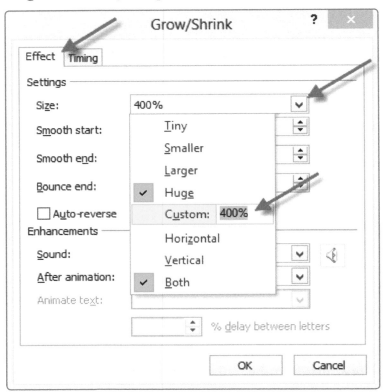

11. Repeat, inserting additional motion paths for all pans and zooms desired.

Lesson 16

Inserting Video

While we typically think of using PowerPoint to show text, photographs, documents, charts, or illustrations, the information that we may need to show sometimes comes in the form of video content. If a picture is worth a thousand words, then perhaps a video is worth ten thousand! Sometimes the best way to get a jury or audience to understand an important point is to play a video or show the evidence to them directly. This is very understandable in the case of video-recorded deposition testimony. By showing a clip or series of clips, you can demonstrate many critical points that would never come through in a still picture or by reading a transcript. Here are a few examples of things that a video deposition may convey, that a still photo or deposition transcript does not:

- periods of silence
- pregnant pauses
- the length of time it takes a deponent to think about and answer a question
- body language (nervous motions or face twitching, facial expressions, sweating, etc.)
- eye movement
- shaky voice

1. On a blank slide, go to the ***Insert*** ribbon and select ***Video***. Browse
   to the location of the video, select it, and click ***Insert***. These steps are
   shown below in Figure 16.1. Note: The most versatile video format
   to use is MPG. You can request MPEG1 from your videographer.

Figure 16.1 Selecting and Inserting a Video

2. Resize the video frame using the corner handles.
3. To adjust the start and end times of the video, right-click on the
   video and select ***Trim Video***, as shown in Figure 16.2.

Figure 16.2 Trim Video

4. Adjust the start time and end time using the green and red sliders and click **OK** (see Figure 16.3).

Figure 16.3 Adjusting Start and End Time of Video

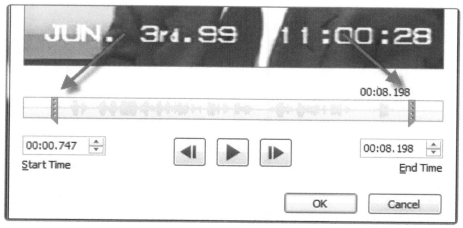

IMPORTANT

If you are using PowerPoint 2007 or earlier, you will not be able to trim the video. This feature is only available in PowerPoint 2010 or later.

WARNING

If you are using PowerPoint 2007 or earlier, the video is *not* embedded within the presentation. To the contrary, it is inserted as a hyperlinked file. When transferring the presentation to another computer, be sure to copy the underlying linked videos. You can easily bundle these files together using the **Package for CD** function:

---

1. Open the presentation in PowerPoint.
2. Select *File > Publish > Package for CD* (even though you may save it to a flash drive or other location).
3. Click *Options* and choose the following:
   - Make package by using original file formats
   - Include Linked files (essential to get the videos)
   - Embedded TrueType fonts (important if you have purchased fonts that do not come with PowerPoint by default)
4. Click *OK* to get back to the Package for CD dialog box.
5. Instead of saving to CD, save to a file location. You can actually save to CD, a flash drive, or a location on your computer or network.
6. To start the presentation, open the folder that it created with all the necessary files and linked files and double-click on the PPT or PPTX file.

Inserting an Audio File or Sound

Using audio or video is a great way to wake everyone up in a presentation. Audio by itself is kind of rare, so I tend to think of it as unique, giving the audience a mental break from visual stimuli. Unique is good. People get bored with PowerPoint like they get bored with any one type of media. Playback of an audio recording mixes things up. Besides, as with video, playing an audio recording is just sometimes necessary to effectively communicate the information or issue that you to need to convey. For instance, you may need to play back an audio clip of an expert's lecture, a telephone recording, a 911 call, or the like.

Inserting an Audio Recording

1. Go to the *Insert* ribbon and select *Audio*, as shown in Figure 17.1.

Figure 17.1 Selecting Audio from Insert Ribbon

> **NOTE**
>
> The most common formats are MP3, MPA, or WAV. You will have to convert your sound file to one of those formats if you have a 911 call or a recorded message that you would like to play back. You can use a program like Cakewalk Pyro (www.cakewalk.com) or Audacity (http://audacity.sourceforge.net/) to convert an analog tape to digital and make edits.

2. Locate and select the desired audio file and click **OK** (see Figure 17.2).

Figure 17.2 Selecting an Audio File

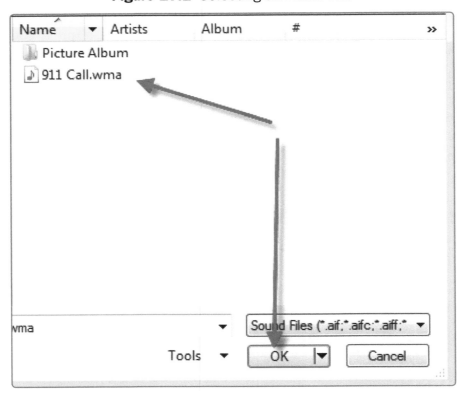

3. To adjust the start and end times of the audio, right-click on the sound file and select *Trim Audio* (see Figure 17.3).

4. Adjust the start time and end time using the green and red sliders (see Figure 17.4) and click *OK*.

Figure 17.3 Trim Audio

Figure 17.4 Adjusting Start and End Time of Audio

5. After inserting the sound file, you may want to add a picture, a label, or an appropriate background to the slide to provide context.

TIP

It can be very effective to have a photograph of the person(s) speaking, along with a text box caption labeling the person(s) speaking, to accompany the audio file. This allows the jury or audience to associate a face with a voice and, at the very minimum, provides some context.

- For a 911 call, insert a photograph of the accident scene if you have one.
- For a lecture, insert a photograph of the person speaking.
- For an audio recording that occurred in the lunchroom at ABC Company, insert a picture of the room or ABC's building. Alternatively, insert a photograph of each person who is speaking.

Inserting and Playing Music with Slides

With the exception of courtroom presentations, it is often effective to set a slide show to music and have the music run automatically. This is good for several kinds of situations:

- photo album presentations
- award presentations
- office celebrations
- office anniversaries

After inserting all your slides (a photo album is an efficient way of doing this) and placing them in the desired order, follow these steps:

1. Go to the first slide where you want the music to start.

2. Select **Insert > Audio from File** (see Figure 17.5).

Figure 17.5 Selecting a Music File

3. Navigate to the desired music file and click *Insert*, as shown in Figure 17.6.

Figure 17.6 Inserting a Music File

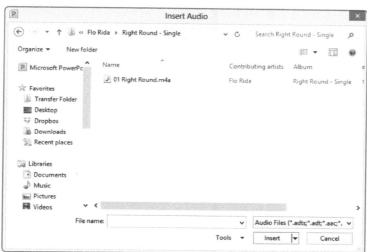

4. Select the sound icon so the contextual ribbon **Playback** is accessible (see Figure 17.7).

Figure 17.7 Accessing the Playback Ribbon

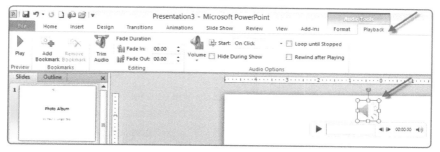

5. Select *Play across slides* and *Loop until Stopped* (see Figure 17.8) so the music will play continuously until the PowerPoint slide show is terminated.

Figure 17.8 Setting Music to Play Continuously

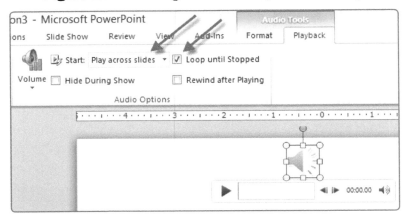

6. If you want to have the slides automatically run, go to the *Transitions* ribbon. In the Timing group on the far right of the ribbon, under **Advance Slide**, deselect *On Mouse Click* and select *After* (see Figure 17.9). Set the number of seconds between each slide. For instance, if you have a sixty-second piece of music and ten slides, you may want to apply six seconds to each. Select *Apply to All* after setting the number of seconds.

Figure 17.9 Setting Slides to Run Automatically

Inserting Excel Spreadsheets and Charts

Excel can be an excellent source of data charts, bar charts, pie charts, and so on. There are several ways to insert an Excel spreadsheet into a Power-Point presentation:

- Create new: Spreadsheet is created from scratch and embedded in the PowerPoint slide. It is not hyperlinked to an external spreadsheet.

- Create from file: Spreadsheet already exists and then is embedded in the PowerPoint slide. It is not hyperlinked to the source spreadsheet.

- Create from file and Link: Spreadsheet already exists and then is embedded as a hyperlink in the PowerPoint slide. Therefore it is updated whenever there are changes in either location.

Inserting New Spreadsheet into PowerPoint

This procedure will create a brand-new spreadsheet from scratch and embed it in the PowerPoint slide. The file is not hyperlinked to an external spreadsheet. It exists solely within PowerPoint.

1. On the **Insert** ribbon, select *Object*. Then select *Microsoft Work-sheet > Create new > OK*. These steps are shown in Figure 18.1.

Figure 18.1 Inserting New Spreadsheet into PowerPoint

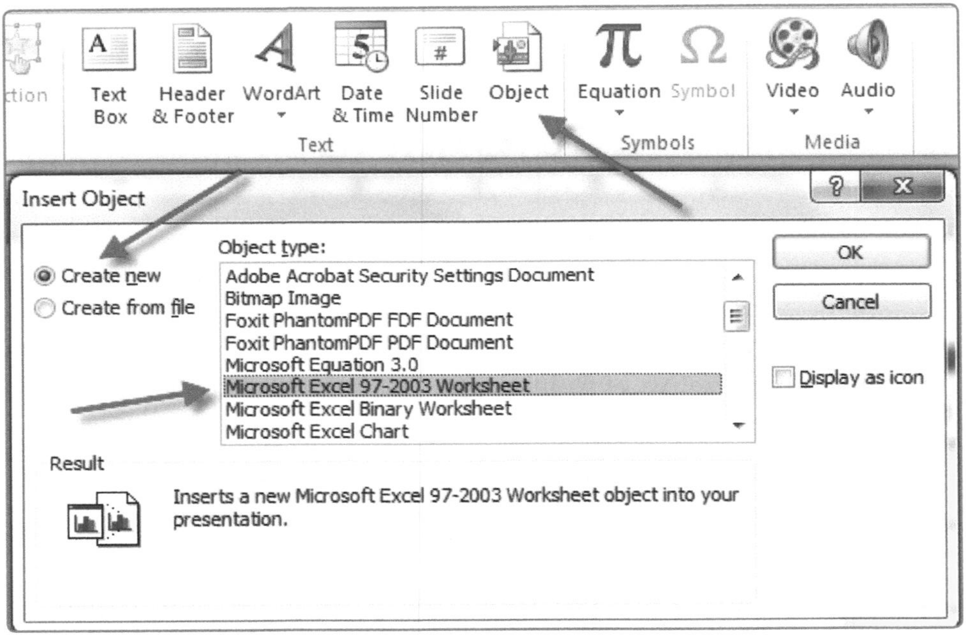

Inserting Existing Spreadsheet into PowerPoint (from File)

This procedure will embed an existing spreadsheet into the PowerPoint slide. The file is not hyperlinked to the source external spreadsheet. It exists as a copy of the original within PowerPoint. In other words, if changes are made in one, those changes will not be reflected in the other.

1. On the **Insert** ribbon, select ***Object***. Then select ***Microsoft Work-sheet > Create from file > Browse to select the spreadsheet > OK***. The steps are shown in Figure 18.2.

Figure 18.2 Inserting Existing Spreadsheet into PowerPoint

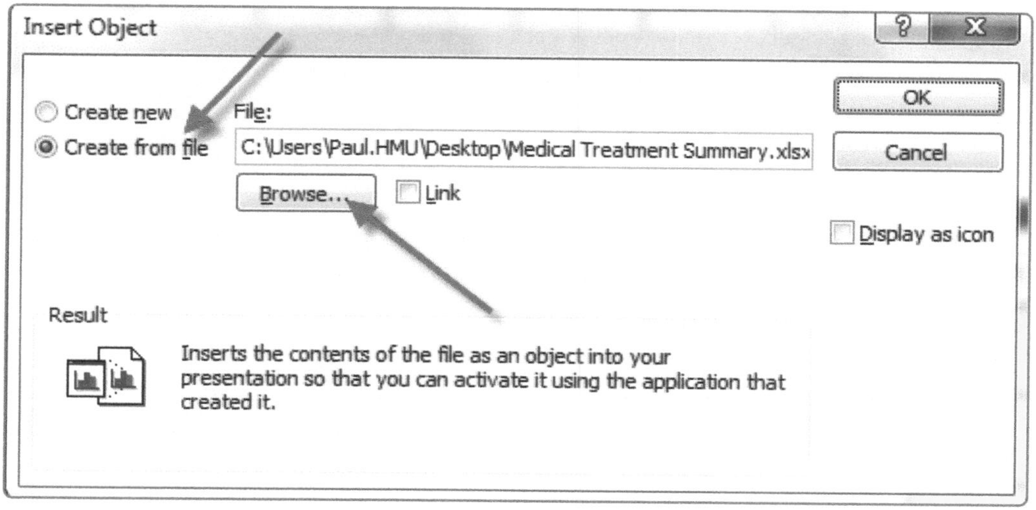

Inserting Existing Spreadsheet as Hyperlink into PowerPoint

This procedure will embed an existing spreadsheet in the PowerPoint slide, hyperlinked to the source external spreadsheet. In other words, if changes are made in one, those changes will be reflected in the other.

1. On the **Insert** ribbon, select ***Object***. Then select ***Microsoft Work-sheet > Create from file > Browse to select the spreadsheet***.

2. Check the **Link** box, as shown in Figure 18.3 and then **OK**.

Figure 18.3 Inserting Existing Spreadsheet into PowerPoint with Hyperlink

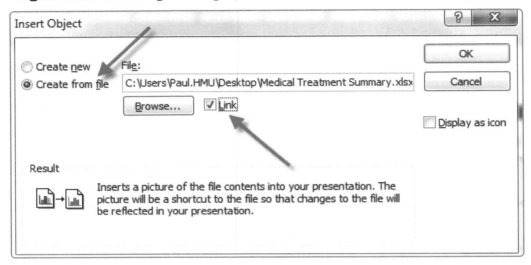

Inserting Excel Chart into PowerPoint

Just like you can insert an Excel spreadsheet into a PowerPoint slide, you can also insert a bar or pie chart created in Excel. Charts allow people to see trends that they may not see from looking at numbers alone. As with spreadsheets, you can import an existing chart or create a brand-new chart. I recommend that you create a new chart in Excel and then bring it into PowerPoint.

1. In Excel, create a pie chart. The example in Figure 18.4 has two rows of data showing client sources. Highlight the data and then go to the **Insert** ribbon and select **Pie.** A pop-up box will show different options for display. I like the 3-D option, which is highlighted in Figure 18.4.

Figure 18.4 Creating a Pie Chart in Excel for PowerPoint

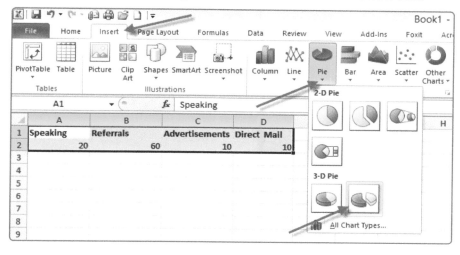

2. Excel will insert the pie chart into the worksheet, as shown in Figure 18.5.

Figure 18.5 Pie Chart in Worksheet

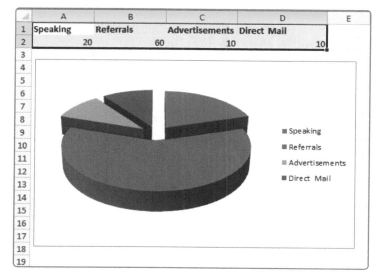

3. Right-click on the border of the chart and select *Copy* (see Figure 18.6).

Figure 18.6 Copying an Excel Chart

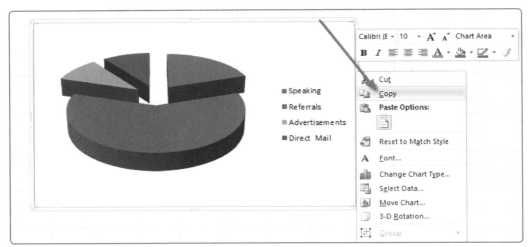

4. In PowerPoint, right-click anywhere on the blank slide and you will see five different paste options, shown as icons (see Figure 18.7). From left to right, they are as follows:
   - Use Destination Theme & Embed Workbook
   - Keep Source Formatting & Embed Workbook
   - Use Destination Theme & Link Data
   - Keep Source Formatting & Link Data

Destination Theme is the theme found in the PowerPoint that you are currently assembling. **Source Formating** is the formatting from the file from which you are copying.

Figure 18.7 Paste Options for Excel Chart

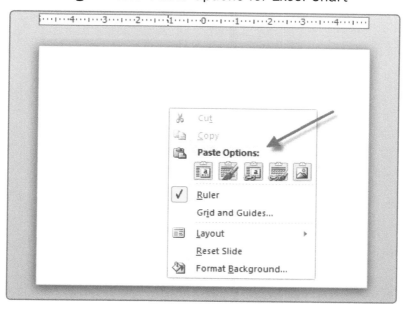

Lesson 19

Creating Time Lines

PowerPoint is great for creating and presenting time lines, but rarely do you find instruction on how to make them. It certainly isn't the easiest way to create a time line,[1] but if done correctly, the payoff is great. There are truly countless ways to design your PowerPoint time line, limited only by your creativity. If you are just starting out, however, you may want to try some of the basic templates that are available from Microsoft.[2]

I like using PowerPoint for time lines for many reasons. First, by displaying one chronological item at a time, I can keep people from reading ahead and better focus everyone's attention on the important point that I want to make. Second, I can create time lines and, if desired, bring them to a reprographics shop to print as blowups on foam board. Third, I and my staff are in total control of edits, which allows for last-minute changes without having to pay a graphic designer. Fourth, in court, once I have finished introducing the time line, I can leave the blowup(s) on an easel for the jury to ground themselves as they hear testimony. This has the added benefit of freeing up PowerPoint for other graphics.

The biggest mistake that I see people make with PowerPoint time lines is that the text is too small. You need to be very careful to design the time

---

1. For those without the time to create a PowerPoint–based time line, some alternatives are TimeMap by LexisNexis or Timeline 3D for the iPad.

2. See http://office.microsoft.com/en-us/templates/timeline-TC001016265.aspx.

line in such a way that the text is large enough to read. Following the 8H rule, discussed in Lesson 2, you should never use a font smaller than 11 points. Typically, my goal is to use 18-point font (or higher) in time lines, although it isn't always possible. This means that you may have to break up your time line across multiple slides. There is nothing wrong with that, and you have to do it if you use the foam board blowups. Your time line is worthless if someone can't see it.

Finally, when designing your PowerPoint time line, try to make it interactive by inserting full-size photographs and documents with callouts. The following example uses this technique.

Building Your Time Line

1. To build a time line, create a horizontal line across the slide, and label the start and end date using text boxes. To create a line, select **Insert > Shapes > Lines**, as shown in Figure 19.1.

Figure 19.1 Creating a Line in PowerPoint

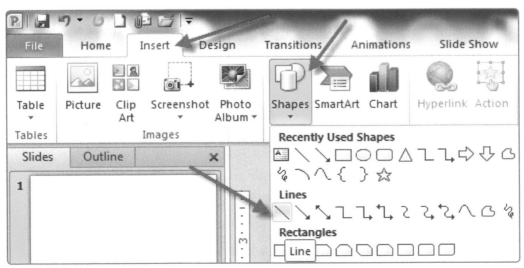

Draw the line across the slide, as seen in Figure 19.2:

Figure 19.2 Line Drawn on PowerPoint Slide

You should create a fairly bold or thick line, and you can add termination points or graphics, if desired. With the line selected, right-click and choose **Format Shape**. In the dialog box, click **Line Style** and then pick a thick width, such as 6 points. Finally, under the arrow settings, select the desired beginning and ending type. These steps are shown in Figure 19.3.

Figure 19.3 Adding Termination Points to Line

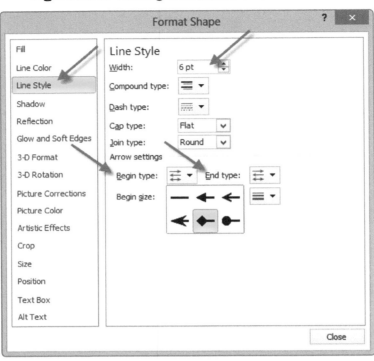

2. Type each date in its own text box (***Insert > Text Box***) and position the text boxes appropriately on the time line (See Lesson 11, "Text Boxes"). Format the text color and size as desired. An example is shown in Figure 19.4. I recommend creating the first text box and then

Figure 19.4 Date Placed on Line

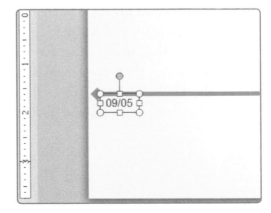

copying and pasting it as many times as needed, just changing the text within the box so you don't have to reinvent the wheel.

3. Next, you are ready to build the "post and banner." Insert a vertical line (the post) approximately 4 points thick, using the methods in step 1. Then insert a rectangle or rounded rectangle shape, formatted with the desired fill color and line color. (See Lesson 12 if you need to review in detail the step-by-step process of inserting and formatting shapes.) Using your mouse or cursor/arrow keys, drag or nudge the shapes to line up with the dates that you inserted in step 2. See Figure 19.5 for an example.

4. Add text to the rectangle (the banner) by simply clicking on it and then typing. You do *not* have to create a separate text box and lay it on top of the rectangle. Format the text appropriately. The example in Figure 19.6 shows white text on a blue background.

Figure 19.5 Vertical Line and Rectangle Inserted for Time Line

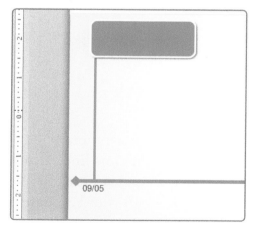

Figure 19.6 Formatted Banner for Time Line

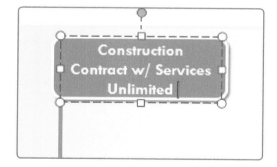

5. Next, and this is an important time-saver, duplicate the slide now that you have all the essential parts to the time line. To do this, select ***Home > New Slide > Duplicate Selected Slides***, as shown in Figure 19.7 below. Keep this slide only as long as you need it to finish your time line and then delete or hide it.

Figure 19.7 Duplicating the Time Line Slide

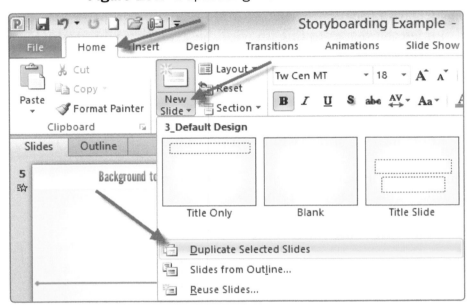

6. Group the date, post, and banner so all the objects can move together if you need to reposition the point on the time line. Also, this will allow you to easily animate all three objects at once. To group the three objects, hold the ***Ctrl*** key down on your keyboard and left-click on each object. Right-click on any one of the objects and select ***Group > Group*** (see Figure 19.8).

Figure 19.8 Grouping Objects

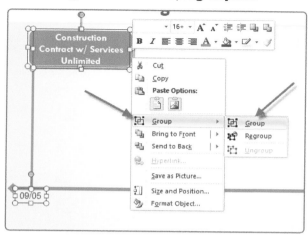

7. Animate the grouped objects by selecting the group. From the **Animations** ribbon, select ***Add Animation*** and then ***More Entrance Effects***, as shown in Figure 19.9.

8. Select ***Strips*** as the entrance effect (see Figure 19.10).

Figure 19.9 Animating a Group

Figure 19.10 Strips Entrance Effect

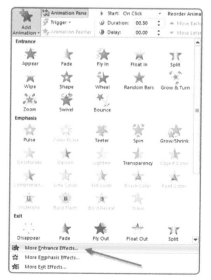

9. Finally, under **Effect Options**, change the direction to **Right Up** (see Figure 19.11). The group of objects will come in from the bottom, but the Strips effect will start with the date. Then the post will swipe up, followed by the banner swiping from left to right. It is a very cool effect.

Figure 19.11 Right Up Effects Option

10. Build the next chronological point by copying from your duplicated slide and pasting it into this slide. Adjust the date, height of the pole, and the text within the banner. Group the objects together and repeat steps 7 through 9. Figure 19.12 shows a time line in progress.

Figure 19.12 Partially Completed Time Line

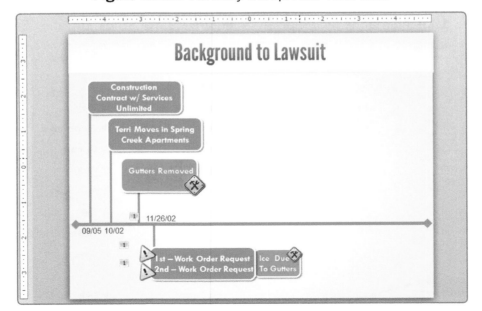

If you want to include pictures or documents after various dates, insert a slide with that content immediately after the slide that you are building. To pick up where you left off, duplicate the slide with the time line and move it to the slide immediately following the photo or document. Before building your next chronological point, open the ***Animation Pane*** in the newly duplicated slide and remove all the animation effects (not the objects), as shown in Figure 19.13. This will force the objects to appear as static when the slide is presented. In other words, you do not want to have to step through all the animated objects in that slide. You just want to build and present the next chronological data point and then animate it.

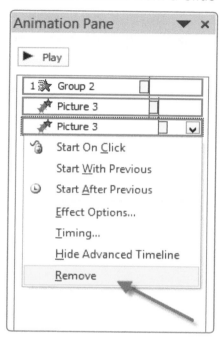

Figure 19.13 Removing Animation Effects from a Slide

Lesson 20

Using Slide Transitions

To give your presentation a polished appearance, you can apply what is called a transition—a pushing or wiping effect between slides. You can add transitions such as a checkerboard, sliding, fading, or many other professional-looking options.

1. Select the desired slide or slides. If you want to apply the same transition to all the slides, use *Ctrl+A* while in the **Slide Sorter** view.

2. On the **Transitions** ribbon, find the transition you want to use (Wipe is the example in Figure 20.1), left-click on it, and then select *Apply to All*.

Figure 20.1 Choosing a Transition

3. PowerPoint will show you a preview of the transition so you can determine if you really want that particular one. If you do not like it, undo by using the Quick Access Toolbar or *Ctrl+Z*.

Lesson 21

Reordering Slides

Rearranging the Order in Slide Sorter View

Once you have your slides built, you may want to move them around.
PowerPoint provides a very easy way to do this in the Slide Sorter view.

1. On the **View** ribbon, select ***Slide Sorter*** (see Figure 21.1). In
   this view, you can drag and drop slides to arrange them in the
   desired order.

Figure 21.1 Slide Sorter View

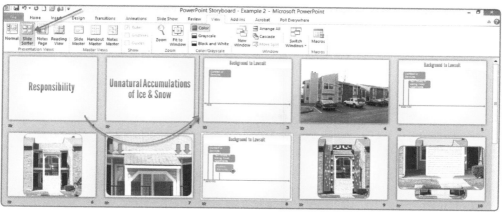

2. To save your changes, use the Quick Access Toolbar or ***Ctrl+S***.

Organizing PowerPoint Slides and Your Thoughts Using Sections

One very effective way to organize your slides and think through your presentation is to create sections within the Slide Sorter view. As shown in Figure 21.2, you can use a section header to capture the slides that are relevant to that section. You can also collapse/hide or expand/show sections, as with folders in Windows Explorer, so you can view only the section with the slides that you want to see.

Figure 21.2 Example of Sections and Section Headers

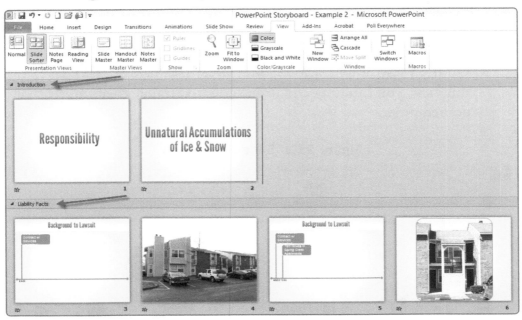

1. Right-click in the open area to the left of the first slide in your section and select **Add Section**, as shown in Figure 21.3.

Figure 21.3 Add Section

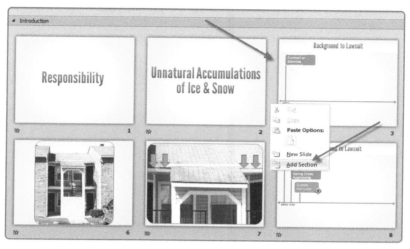

2. A new untitled section will appear. Right-click on it and select **Rename Section** (see Figure 21.4). Enter the section name and click **Rename**.

Figure 21.4 Naming a Section

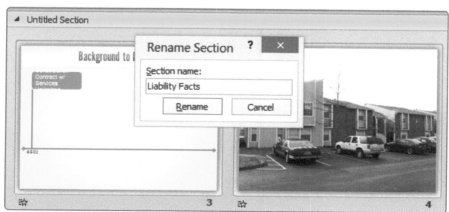

Dual Monitors and Presenter View

I strongly recommend connecting to a projector or large-screen monitor and using dual extending displays. This allows you to see your notes and upcoming slides on a primary monitor, such as your laptop, while everyone else is looking at the big screen. It is the perfect way to let you remove a lot of the text from slides that probably belongs in your notes. For example, in Figure 22.1, the audience sees only the slide that is shown on the left. The presenter sees that slide as well as any notes and upcoming slides.

Figure 22.1 Presenter's View of Slide Show

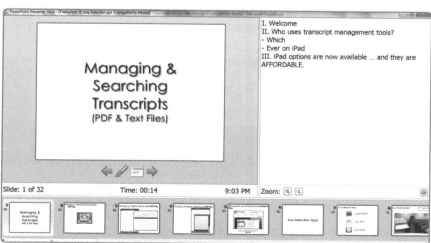

Setting Up Presenter View

1. First, connect the projector or large LCD monitor to your laptop. Next, turn on the projector or monitor. Right-click on your Windows desktop and select ***Screen resolution***, as shown in Figure 22.2.

Figure 22.2 Selecting Screen Resolution on Desktop

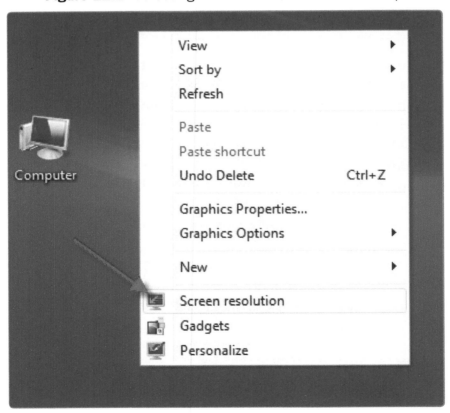

2. In the dialog box (see Figure 22.3), set the option for multiple displays to ***Extend these displays***.

Figure 22.3 Setting Multiple Displays

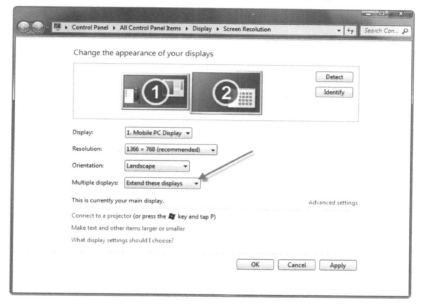

3. In PowerPoint, on the **Slide Show** ribbon, select *Use Presenter View*. For the **Show On** option, choose *Monitor 2*. Both of these steps are shown in Figure 22.4.

Figure 22.4 Setting Presenter View and Choosing Monitor

When you start your presentation, the projector or large LCD monitor will show only your slides, but your laptop monitor will show Presenter view, which gives you the ability to see the current slide, your notes, and the slides that are coming up. You can even skip around in the presentation if needed. Your screen will look similar to the one in Figure 22.1.

Slide Show Delivery

Jumping around in PowerPoint Presentations

You can jump around in a slide presentation by simply typing the slide number and hitting **_Enter_**. For instance, if you want to jump from slide 5 to slide 25, just type 25 and press the Enter key. (Note: You will not see the number appear as you type it.) This technique comes in handy if you run out of time and want to quickly skip a set of slides. However, you need to know the slide numbers to do this effectively. This generally requires that you either print the slides with numbers (see below) or memorize them. Memorization can be risky.

Last-minute changes to a presentation can really mess up your slide numbers. For this reason, I recommend hiding slides at the last minute as opposed to deleting them. This will preserve the slide numbers, but the slides will not be displayed. You know a slide is hidden if there is a slash through the slide number (see Figure 23.1).

Figure 23.1 Number on a Hidden Slide

To hide a slide, right-click on it and select *Hide Slide*. You can use the same procedure to redisplay a hidden slide, as shown in Figure 23.2.

Figure 23.2 Redisplaying a Hidden Slide

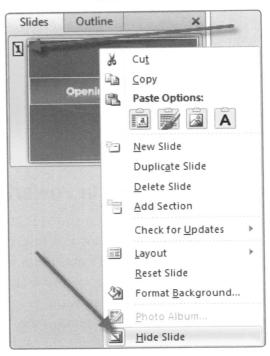

Inserting and Showing Slide Numbers

If you use the above technique of skipping slides, it may be helpful to have the slide numbers handy on a printout or visible on the slides.

1. To insert slide numbers, select *Insert > Slide Number* (see Figure 23.3).

Figure 23.3 Inserting Slide Numbers

2. In the dialog box that appears, check *Slide number*. Check *Don't show on title slide* if you do not want a slide number to appear on the first slide. Then select *Apply to All*. These steps are shown in Figure 23.4.

Figure 23.4 Setting Slide Numbers

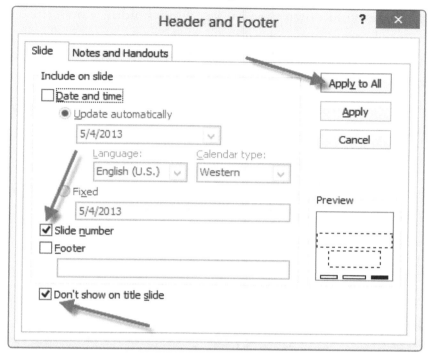

Presentation Tips

- To present a slide show, select either *From Beginning* or *From Current Slide* (see Figure 23.5) on the **Slide Show** ribbon, depending on what slide you want to show first.

Figure 23.5 Setting the Start of a Slide Show

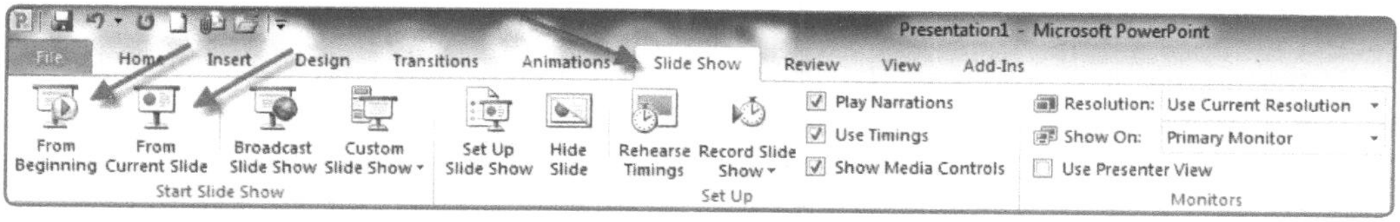

- To turn the mouse pointer into a laser pointer in the slide show, press and hold down the Ctrl key while holding down the left mouse button and moving the mouse.
- To advance to the next slide, you can use the space bar, Page Up key, or the left mouse button.
- To go back to the previous slide, you can use the Backspace key or the Page Down key.
- To add slide timings, select *Rehearse Timings* on the **Slide Show** ribbon (see Figure 23.5). Navigate through your slide show, and pause on each slide for the amount of time needed during your actual presentation. Click Yes to save the rehearsal timings.
- To black out the screen, hit the B key.
- To white out the screen, hit the W key.

Presentation Keystrokes

Keystroke	Function
F5	Start slide show from beginning
Shift+F5	Start slide show from current slide
N Enter Space bar Right or down arrow Page Down	Next slide or animation
P Backspace Left or up arrow Page Up	Previous slide or animation
Slide number + Enter	Move to specific slide number
Esc	Cancel slide show

Keystroke	Function
B	Black out presentation (B again to restore)
W	White out presentation (W again to restore)
Home	Jump to first slide
Hold both mouse buttons for two seconds	Jump to first slide
End	Jump to last slide
S	Stop (or restart) automatically running slide show
Shift+F10	Display menu
Ctrl+P	Display pen on screen
E	Erase on-screen annotations
Ctrl+H	Hide mouse pointer
A	Show or hide mouse pointer
Ctrl+P	Change mouse pointer to pen
Ctrl+A	Change mouse pointer to arrow
Ctrl+E	Change mouse pointer to eraser
Ctrl + hold left mouse button	Change mouse pointer to laser pointer
Ctrl+M	Show or hide inking
Ctrl+S	Show All Slides dialog menu
Alt+Q	Stop media playback
Alt+P	Toggle play/pause
Alt+Up Arrow	Increase volume
Alt+Down Arrow	Decrease volume
Alt+U	Mute

Presenting PowerPoint on iPads

Presenting PowerPoint from your iPad can result in a more natural and interactive presentation, allowing you to walk around, switch between applications, and write notes or use a whiteboard.

Getting Your PowerPoint Presentation on Your iPad

Since Microsoft doesn't have an app available for the iPad yet, it is currently impossible to display a native PowerPoint slide show on an iPad. You must convert the presentation to an acceptable iPad format and show it with an app that gives you options similar to PowerPoint. Keynote and SlideShark are two excellent products for this purpose.

Keynote is Apple's answer to PowerPoint. When the iPad was released, Apple developed an app for the iPad that costs $9.99 in the App Store. Once your PowerPoint slide show is converted to Keynote, you have the ability to make edits and show the presentation. The downside is that the conversion isn't always perfect. This requires that you make some tweaks and fixes before showing the slides from your iPad.

SlideShark (www.slideshark.com) is a free app that will convert PowerPoint to an iPad-friendly format and then allow you to play/show the slides. It converts PowerPoint better than any other app I have seen, preserving fonts and animations extremely well. It surpasses Keynote at retaining the original formatting. SlideShark also has a fantastic presenter's view that allows you to easily see your notes and upcoming slides, very similar to PowerPoint's Presenter view. See Figure 24.1 for an example.

Figure 24.1 SlideShark Presenter's View

The downside to SlideShark is that you cannot make edits to the slide show from the iPad. You have to make changes in PowerPoint and then convert and upload again. With large presentations and low bandwidth, this can take a few minutes.

Keynote Instructions

The easiest way to convert a PowerPoint presentation to Keynote on your iPad is through Dropbox (or another similar cloud-based storage service with an app for the iPad). Save your PowerPoint in Dropbox. When you tap on the PowerPoint file in Dropbox and it loads in the viewer, tap the *Share* icon and then *Open in* . . . (see Figure 24.2).

Figure 24.2 Opening a PowerPoint File with the Keynote App

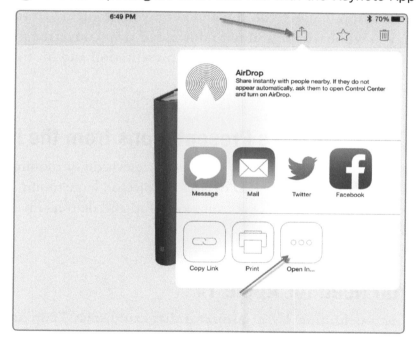

Next select *Keynote* and give it a moment to load and convert the PowerPoint to Keynote. Once opened in Keynote, you can show the slide show via the iPad and the file will be stored locally on your iPad until you delete it.

SlideShark Instructions

Go to www.slideshark.com and set up a free account. This will also set up the necessary cloud storage area for your presentation, which you can link to Dropbox, Box, Google Drive, or Syncplicity. Once the account is created, log in and upload your finished PowerPoint file (or files). During the upload process, SlideShark will convert the file and store it in your private storage area.

Next, from your iPad, go to the App Store and download and install the SlideShark app. Launch the app and enter your login credentials. Once logged in, you will have the ability to download your converted presentation from the SlideShark cloud. Select the presentation and hit the green *Play* button.

Apple TV for Wireless Presentations from the iPad

The first thing to note is that Apple TV is *not* a television or monitor. It is a small box that plugs into your HD device: a projector, large monitor, or TV. It receives the wireless video signal from your iPad and delivers images and video to your HD device.

What You Need for Apple TV

- A high-definition TV or projector that can display 720p or 1080p video
- Apple TV (second or higher), $99 at the Apple Store
- HDMI cable, $10 to $30
- You may need an HDMI-to-VGA converter if you do not have a projector with an HDMI input or if the room where you are presenting has only VGA inputs. This gives a lower quality display

than HDMI, but it works fine and is sometimes essential. The Kanex ATV Pro, $49.95, is one option.

- Buy a wireless router (small or somewhat portable). It is strongly recommended that you do *not* rely on public Wi-Fi, in the court-room or elsewhere. Connectivity is too spotty.

- Here are two products that would work fine, but there are many excellent routers on the market:

    ○ Apple AirPort Extreme 802.11n Dual-Band Wi-Fi Wireless Router, Model A1354, $99

    ○ Linksys Dual N Band Wireless Router, WRT610N 802.11n, $50

Apple TV Setup

1. **Set up the wireless network.** Set up your wireless network with encryption. You may want to have your IT folks do this to save time. If you are adventurous, it isn't difficult. Here are two excellent guides from *PCWorld* that can help:

    - http://www.pcworld.com/article/249185/how_to_set_up_a_wireless_router.html

    - http://www.pcworld.com/article/130330/article.html

    Write down your network name (SSID) and password and keep them in a safe place. You may want to write the SSID and password on a label and affix it to the inside of the router's packing box or Apple TV packing box for convenience.

2. **Connect Apple TV to your television or projector.** Plug in your Apple TV's power cable and then connect Apple TV via the HDMI cable to your HD television or projector. Turn on your television or projector and switch the input to the HDMI source where Apple TV is connected.

3. **Set up AirPlay Password.** Using the Apple TV remote control, under *Settings > AirPlay*, select *On* and add a password. Save the password in a safe location. Write it on a label and affix it to the inside bottom of the Apple TV packing box.

4. **Connect Apple TV to wireless network.** Under *Settings > General > Network*, select *Configure WiFi*. Choose your wireless network from the list and enter your network password. It may take a couple of minutes to establish a connection.

5. **Turn off Apple TV screen saver.** Under *Settings > Screen Saver*, select *Never*. This will prevent Apple TV from showing wild animals in the middle of your presentation in the event that it sits idle for more than five minutes!

6. **Connect your iPad to Apple TV.** Double-click on the iPad *Home* button so it reveals the multitasking dock at the bottom. Swipe the dock to the right. You will see an additional button with an icon for AirPlay (see Figure 24.3). Tap on the *AirPlay* button, select your Apple TV, and turn *Mirroring* to the *On* position. In a few seconds, you should see your iPad displayed on your large screen.

Figure 24.3 Activating AirPlay

7. **Have a backup plan for wired setup.** Always have a backup plan! In the event something goes wrong, always have your iPad-to-VGA adapter and iPad-to-HDMI adapter so you can plug your iPad directly into your television or projector. Bring both adapters every time. One can never be too paranoid or cautious when planning for presentations. The adapters cost approximately $49 each and can be purchased at the Apple Store at http://store.apple.com/us/ipad/ipad-accessories/cables-docks#! or through other online vendors.

Additional Resources

Official Apple TV setup guide

http://manuals.info.apple.com/en_US/apple_tv_3rd_gen_setup.pdf

Kanex ATV Pro HDMI-to-VGA Adapter

http://www.kanexlive.com/atvpro, $69

This adapter retails for $69, but can be found for under $50 from many resellers on the web.

Themes, Master Slides, and Templates

Some of PowerPoint's standard design schemes are very good. However, they tend to be overused, and many have distracting graphics that can interfere with pictures, video, documents, and other displays that are used quite frequently in legal presentation. For this reason, it is a good idea to create a customized design, especially with your own firm logo and colors. It is very easy to create a professional-looking title slide. Before we begin, let's review some basic terminology.

Theme. A PowerPoint theme stores design elements such as colors, fonts, and background graphics. A theme gives you the flexibility of being able to apply those elements to a single slide, selected slides, or an entire presentation. You can save a theme so you do not have to redo all the work you did to put together a design for a presentation that you like. The theme would not store the content (words, pictures, user-created graphics, etc.) of slides but could store color and fonts. It is best to modify the Slide Master (see below) before saving the theme so slides are more consistent. Themes are accessed in the Themes gallery (see Figure 25.1) on the **Design** ribbon. They are THMX files.

Figure 25.1 Themes Gallery on Design Ribbon

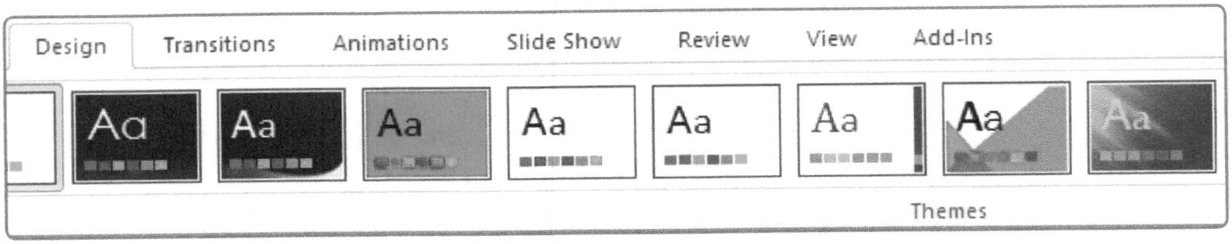

Slide Master. The PowerPoint Slide Master is a set of slides that store information about font styles, placeholder positions, background designs, and color schemes. One typically modifies the Slide Master when saving themes and templates. You access the Slide Master from the **View** ribbon, as shown in Figure 25.2.

Figure 25.2 Slide Master on View Ribbon

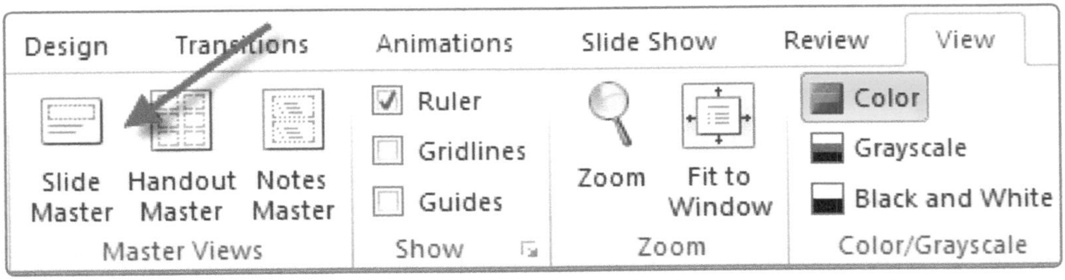

Template. A PowerPoint template, like a theme, can store design elements such as colors, fonts, and graphics. However, templates can also store slide content such as text, pictures, flowcharts, and other items. Access templates via **File > New > My templates** (see Figure 25.3) or **Available templates**.

Figure 25.3 PowerPoint Templates

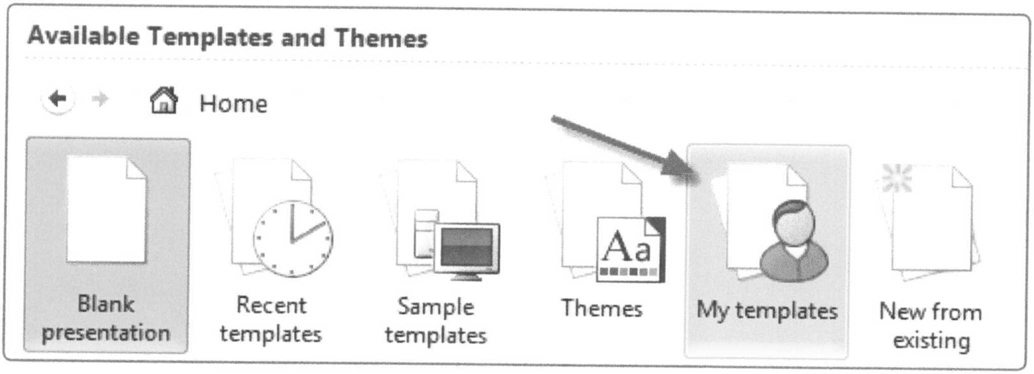

Using a Theme

If using an already created PowerPoint presentation, you may want to work with a copy just to be safe.

Click on the ***Design*** ribbon and select one of the themes (see Figure 25.4).

Figure 25.4 Design Ribbon and Themes

IMPORTANT NOTE

If you do not have a slide or set of slides selected, the theme will be applied to every slide in your presentation. It is generally recommended that you apply a theme when you first create the presentation so that you do not accidentally overwrite any custom colors and fonts in your existing slideshow. There are many themes to select. The gallery in Figure 25.4 shows some of the variety.

Saving a Theme

If using an already created presentation, you should save a copy of it and work with the copy before saving the theme. You may also want to make modifications to the Slide Master (see below) to ensure desired and consistent results when applying the theme later.

1. After customizing the colors, fonts, and design, select *File > Save As* and then save as *Office Theme* (see Figure 25.5).

Figure 25.5 Saving a Theme

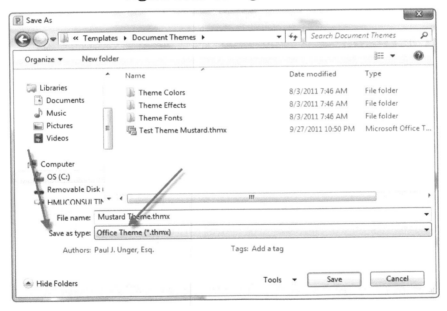

2. Alternatively, you could select the drop-down menu from the Themes gallery (see Figure 25.6) and select *Save Current Theme* (see Figure 25.7).

Figure 25.6 Drop-Down Menu in Themes Gallery

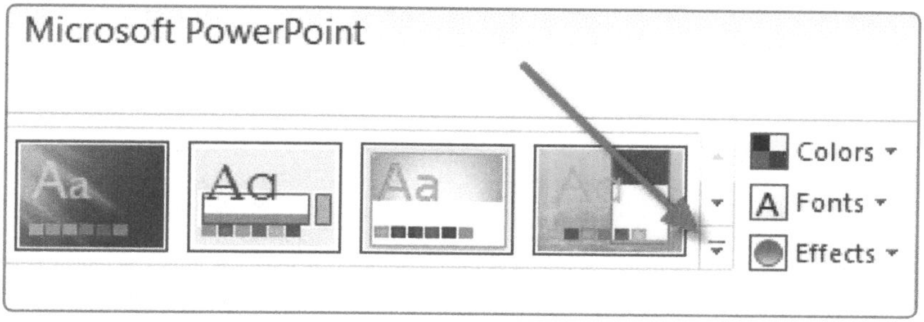

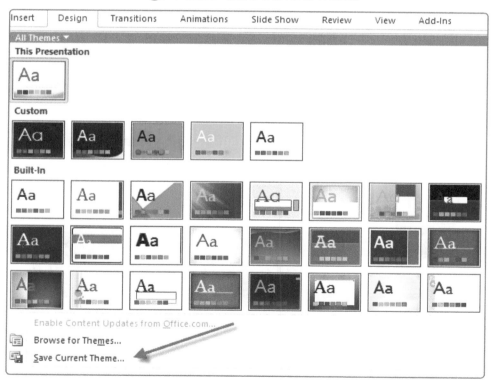

Figure 25.7 Save Current Theme

Modifying the Slide Master

1. On the **View** ribbon, select ***Slide Master*** (see Figure 25.8).

Figure 25.8 Slide Master on View Ribbon

2. It is within this view (editing mode) that you can change fonts, colors, and backgrounds and move placeholders around (see Figure 25.9).

Figure 25.9 Slide Master (Editing Mode)

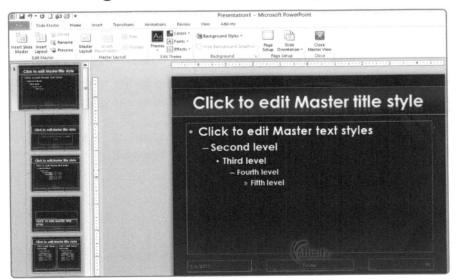

3. Making a change to Slide 1 will affect all the slides that are a subset of it. In other words, you probably want to change the first slide so it makes a universal change, as opposed to changing every single slide below it. Slide 1 is pictured in Figure 25.10 with the red arrow.

Figure 25.10 Slide 1 in Slide Master

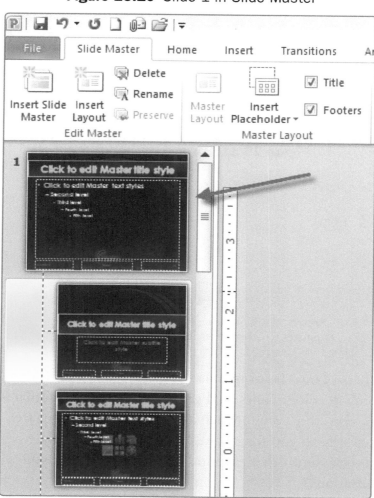

4. I recommend making the following edits:

   a. Change the background to your desired color and gradient or insert a custom background (see Lesson 5, "Inserting Custom Graphic as Background").

   b. Change the font color and size. Be sure to change the fonts at all levels.

   c. Add any custom text boxes and placeholders.

Using a Template

Template (POT or POTX) files are found and accessed at *File > New > My templates* (see Figure 25.11) or *Available templates*.

Figure 25.11 PowerPoint Templates

Remember, a PowerPoint template, like a theme, can store design elements such as colors, fonts, and graphics. However, templates, unlike themes, can also store content such as text, pictures, flowcharts, and other items. So one reason you may want to use or save a template is if you have language/text or some other graphics in a slide show that you will use in other presentations.

Saving a Template

1. After customizing the Slide Master, colors, fonts, and design, select *File > Save As* and then save as *PowerPoint Template* (see Figure 25.12).

Figure 25.12 Saving a Template

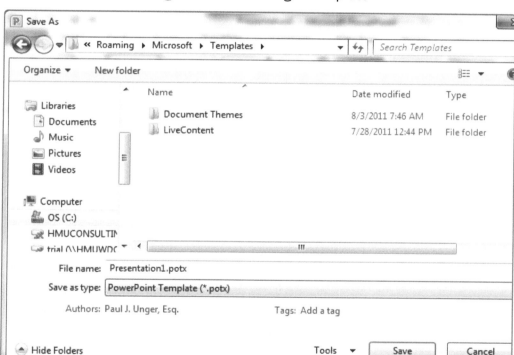

Index

Note: For page numbers followed by "f," the reference is in a figure.